Treasured TIMES

101 CREATIVE GIFT IDEAS UNDER $10

Along with 101 Memorable Gift Ideas Shared by Others

Lonna Weidemann

D1472810

Treasured Times
© 2004 by Lonna Weidemann

First printing 2004
Printed in the United States of America.

ISBN 0-9748316-2-X

Copy Editing by Customline Wordware
Book Design, Typography and Cover by Bookcovers.com

FOR MY MOM

ACKNOWLEDGEMENTS

Giving has always been a passion of mine and I attribute that to my wonderful mother, who always acknowledged the good things I did. Her support has inspired me~

A special thank you to my husband for never doubting me and supporting me with all my crazy ideas~

To Shelby and Dylan, my patient children, for listening and saying my ideas are "cool!"

All my dear friends for lending an ear over and over again!

Lastly, to all of the wonderful people in the world who have poured out their hearts with their truly meaningful gift ideas.

TABLE OF CONTENTS

CHAPTER ONE: GIFTS FOR FRIENDS

If anyone deserves a gift, it's a friend. These are the people who are always there for us, ready to lend a hand or a sympathetic shoulder to cry on.

But they can also be the hardest people to find gifts for! People that you see often are the ones that challenge your creativity.

Don't worry: help is here! In the next few pages, you'll find wonderful ideas that will stimulate your own creative thinking and will inspire your friends as well.

BROWN BAG LUNCH

Treat your friend to a brown bag lunch on their birthday! Fix up a special sandwich and treats to eat throughout the day. This idea is also great for men and co-workers. The day before, give the recipient a note that reads, "Your birthday lunch is covered. Homemade by me!" Fill the bag to the top with extra fun snacks such as jerky, fruit snacks and drinks (including boxed or bottled juices). Here are a few more items you can add:

- Boiled Eggs
- Sliced Veggies and Ranch Dip
- Rolled Tortilla Sandwich
- Mixed Nuts
- Pasta Salad
- Cheese and Crackers
- Bagels or Muffins

I once received a coupon caddy loaded with coupons. My sister used to give me hand-made coupons also. These were for a whole range of different things, from babysitting to going to the store for me, washing my car, etc. She gave them to me for my birthday and it was a gift that I used all year. Some were really funny and cute, written on a plain 3x5 card and well-decorated as well!

- DENISE DELSMAN
(DAVIE, FLORIDA)

ORGANIC LOTIONS

Not something you see every day, this is a great treat for a friend! If you have a heath food store in your area, make a special visit. They usually have a cosmetics department where you will find wonderful scented hand and body lotions in large 12 oz. bottles with pumps. Avalon Organic Botanicals carry the wonderful scents of Lavender, Mint Thyme, Rosemary, and Lemon Verbana. Very scented and a great value for under $10.00!

By learning how to make soap and bath products, I always have odds and ends of soaps, bath bombs, bath salts, etc., that I don't need. By using cellophane bags and labels I make myself; I can package even small leftovers or odd bars of soaps to give away for friends to try. It's very low-cost and something from the heart! If you add a small basket, wash cloth or scrub mitt, a few bath bombs, you have a very nice gift.

- DEBBIE KRIVANEC
(DOUGLAS, WYOMING)

INSPIRATIONAL MOMENTS

Greeting cards make great framed art! Take a picture or a poem from a greeting card and put it into a picture frame. It adds a great look to a bedroom or bathroom ledge. If the back of the frame is cardboard, write a personal message to your recipient. Another idea is to make a scrap booking page in the size of 8 1/2" x 11" with a few favorite photos. Instead of adding it to a book, add it to a picture frame!

One gift that I received when I turned 16, was a second-hand framed print, not very big, about 5 x 7, that was given to me by my best friend. It featured a heartfelt poem about friendship. My friend tied it up with a big pink bow and added a simple card. I still have that print today and it's proudly displayed on my hutch! That was over 18 years ago, and I still remember what an effect it had on me. My friend and I have kept in touch through the years, but when I'm feeling down or lost, I reread that poem and I remember that special "teenage" friendship. It really means a lot to me.

- CHRISTINE BEERS
(ATHENS, PENNSYLVANIA)

CANDLE SCENTS

Many women love candles and it doesn't have to be a $30.00 candle set to be a nice gift. Here is a simple and elegant idea: Take a candle and place it on a flat candle-holder or plate. Add a small amount of potpourri around it, or small decorative rocks. You can purchase most of these supplies from Wal-Mart or your local department store. Set it in a cellophane bag and wrap the top with ribbon.

The best gift I ever received was given to me by my best friend. I was chairing our elementary school's yearly carnival. Chairing this event takes over your life for a good six months. Carnival was just a few weeks away and I was completely stressed out about all the last-minute details and problems that had arisen. My friend left me a present by the front door for me to find one afternoon when I arrived home. It was a small box that read, "Stress Relief Kit" on the outside; and inside she had placed two bite-sized chocolate bars and an individual-sized bottle of Crown Royal whiskey. The kit made me laugh and I was very touched that she had thought of me and made me such a special gift. To this day, I have not touched either the chocolate or the whiskey! I keep it in my dresser drawer as a reminder of two things: the thoughtfulness of a wonderful friend and the way the kit symbolizes to me that I can get through any situation. I think of my "stress relief kit" as my back-up; knowing it is there helps me get through my most stressful days!

- SHARON ST.PIERRE
(OLNEY, MARYLAND)

DINNER IN A BAG

This idea features all the fixings for dinner and dessert - in a brown paper bag! Staple it shut and add a bow with a card that reads, "Have dinner on me!" Here are three dinner-in-a-bag versions that are sure to thrill your recipient:

- Cool Summer - Cold cuts, cheese, pita pocket bread, pasta salad, fruit pizza or cookies.
- Romantic Fun - Pizza ingredients, crust, sauce, cheese, toppings, cake or frozen pie for dessert.
- Festive - Tacos, hamburger, shells or tortillas, cheese, tomato, salsa, can of refried beans, plate of brownies.
- Go to www.allrecipes.com for more great ideas!

A recipe with detailed instructions is a great gift for a "mad scientist" in the kitchen!

- ANN TANNER
(NEWPORT BEACH, CALIFORNIA)

Sun Tea Treat

Purchase a sun tea jar (available at most grocery stores for about $4.99). Make some sun tea, add a bow, and voila! For added fun add a lemon to a small cellophane bag and hang it on the jar with ribbon along with a gift tag that reads "A jar of raspberry sun tea for you." Change the flavor of tea that you make for variety.

I went to my local craft store and picked up a bunch of the holiday season coffee mugs. I then got some pretzels, strawberries and melting chocolate. I hand dipped the strawberries and pretzels in the chocolate and filled the mugs with those yummy snacks. I thrilled 20-something people and it cost me less than $50!

- BETH LESHER
(NEWTON FALLS, OHIO)

CRAFT CLASS

Sign your recipient up for an upcoming craft or project class. Many craft stores offer classes and you can inquire about upcoming events. Classes range from five to one hundred dollars. Take the flyer or description of the class and put it in a greeting card, that will feature your gift. When you put a gift in a greeting card, be sure to jazz up the envelope. It only takes a few more minutes. Spell the person's name out with glue and plastic jewels; or wrap the card up in a wide ribbon with a big bow. Consider a craft book along with some supplies as another nice gift (maybe a follow up!). A great source for craft kits and craft supplies is www.createforless.com. (See reference page for additional information.)

One of the most memorable gifts I ever received was actually given to me by two friends. They got together and blew up approximately 30 balloons and then hand wrote wonderful and meaningful notes to me on each of the balloons. It was so awesome to walk in and see the room filled with brightly colored balloons and then read what the girls had written. We were the best of friends and still remain close after many years.

- DEB SOLBERG
(PHOENIX, ARIZONA)

FUN WITH PRETZELS!

A very inexpensive gift that is a delight to make is dipped pretzels! It's a great hit with a lot of people and is so easy to make, you can involve the entire family. Purchase a bag of long stick pretzel rods. Coat the pretzels with melted milk, dark, or white chocolate (located in the baking section at the grocery store).

Then use some of these ideas for toppings: crushed nuts, crushed peppermint, toffee pieces, coconut etc. Melt your chocolate and dip half of the pretzel stick in it. Roll it in the topping mixes that are set on a plate. Once coated, set on waxed paper to dry. Be careful – chocolate dries quite quickly!

Give it a professional look by putting your pretzel stick in a pretzel rod cellophane bag. You can find these bags at www.candylandcrafts.com very inexpensively. Tie the ends with ribbons or twist ties. A fabulous, eye-catching gift for anyone at anytime! Consider putting 6 different pretzels in a mug or cup with a ribbon around it. Fun, Fun, Fun!

A very easy and inexpensive gift to give is a lighted flower arrangement. Simply buy an artificial flower or plant and weave a small strand of lights through it. Leave out some length to the cord so it can be plugged in. It is beautiful and adds a very nice decorative touch to a home.

- JESSICA COBIA
(GULF BREEZE, FLORIDA)

DAZZLE HER WITH JEWELS

Keep your eye out for special savings on jewelry. Believe it or not, you can purchase gold earrings and silver necklaces for as low as $10.00. Many jewelry stores offer specials on items they have purchased in volume. My twelve-year-old daughter often purchases jewelry for her friends for the holidays, as it is an exquisite gift in her price range. Her friends are thrilled and impressed with their gifts.

Starting a "Recipe Memory Book" for someone makes a great gift. Start one for a child who is moving out on their own - with all of their favorite dishes from Mom's kitchen! For a special bridal shower gift, have the bridesmaids and mothers each contribute their favorite recipe to get the memory book started. The gift will cost as much as you want to spend on the book itself, from less than a dollar for a simple spiral-bound notebook to several dollars for a scrapbook-style book. But the type of book isn't nearly as important as always remembering to include the giver's name and the date on the front of the recipe card. Thirty years later, your recipient can go down memory lane, remembering all the wonderful people in his or her life!

- LARRY PFEIL
(NEW YORK, NEW YORK)

HERB POT

Paint a terra cotta pot white, or some bright uplifting color, and add a pretty ribbon around the top of the pot. Plant an herb inside for a great gift. When opening the seed packet, open nicely with scissors. After you have planted the herb, tape the seed packet to a bamboo skewer and add it to the pot, so that the recipient knows what herb it is and how to care for it. Herbs are available at most nurseries and department stores. Consider adding a growing pamphlet or small "how to" book attached to the back of the pot.

Wrap a small empty box in wrapping paper and attach the following on a gift tag:

This is a very special gift
That you can never see.
The reason it's so special is
It's just for you from me.
Whenever you are lonely
Or even feeling blue,
You only have to hold this gift
And know I think of you.
You never can un wrap it.
Please keep the ribbon tied.
Just hold the box close to your heart
It's filled with love inside.

- ALISON RICHMOND
(WEST YORKSHIRE, UK)

BLANK GIFT CARDS

If you are feeling creative, cut some cardstock to make a set of gift cards. Cut out designs for the front out of another color of cardstock, and use items like these to decorate:

- buttons
- ribbon
- string
- twigs
- cinnamon sticks
- dried flowers

Print a simple word or phrase (such as Thank you, For You, Love, etc.) and paste it in the center of the card. An easy card for a male recipient is to use a tan-colored card stock with a piece of jute or twine added to the front. Simply cut a strip, tie it in a knot in the center, and glue the knot onto the card, letting the strings hang.

Wrap each card in a cellophane bag. Make a set of three for a handy gift that a friend is sure to use!

No matter who gives the gift, for what reason, or how expensive it is, a personal note - via pen or keyboard - always means more to me than the gift itself.

This is true with presents, but even more so with a card. Just to know that the giver has thought enough about me to take the time to express the reason behind the gift, gives the whole idea a new and cherished meaning. Anyone can pick out a card that is appropriate for the occasion, there are millions out there, but a personal note says I want this for you.

- LINDA MCNEECE
(PARIS, TEXAS)

CHAPTER TWO: KID'S GIFTS

Okay, admit it: kids are a challenge. What can you get them that will please both them - and their parents? For that matter, what can you give that will last more than five minutes, or not be relegated to the back of a dusty closet?

We've filled the next few pages with lots of ideas for the kids on your list, in your neighborhood, in your house, even - ideas that will delight the child while keeping expenses under control. From toddlers to teens, we've got you covered! Enjoy!

FISHY FUN

Give a goldfish, fish bowl and fish food for a great kid's gift. (Of course, you'll want to first obtain parents' permission!) If you would like the child to pick out their own fish, then give them the bowl, food and a certificate or cash for the fish so they can choose. Many Wal-Mart stores have a pet department where you can purchase inexpensive supplies. You'll also want to include a booklet that will teach the child how to be a responsible fish-keeper.

My most memorable gift is one that I have yet to give. I have two children, and when I became pregnant with each, I decided to write them each a journal. These journals were written throughout the full nine months I was pregnant. They include details of how I met their dad, things about my upbringing, family history, and the ideals I would like to instill in them as they grow up. I also wrote about my goals and what each child means to me. I am very happy and proud that I was able to complete these for each child and one day, when I know it will touch their hearts, I will give it to them.

- LONNA WEIDEMANN
(HELENA, MONTANA)

VIDEO FUN

Make their day by giving them a roll of quarters for video game fun! Wrap your roll of coins in a velvet or mesh gift bag, along with a note explaining what the quarters are for. You may even want to include a date and time when you will take them to the video arcade. Wrap your note in a scroll shape, attaching to the bag with a gold ribbon.

One Christmas, many years ago, my parents had wrapped a HUGE box and I saw it under our tree. When asking for whom it was intended, they replied: "it's a dollhouse for your two little sisters, but don't say anything, it's a secret." My sisters were babies at that time. When we were all done opening presents, that huge box was still there. I asked my parents why. They laughed. They told me to open the box. I did. As I ripped the wrapping, opened the box, all I found was my OLD clothes, including my sisters and parents as well. I started laughing and thought it was a joke. Buried deep down in the old clothes was a radio that I have been wanting and my parents could not afford - but managed to buy to make my dream come true. They had me fooled until the very end. Packaging a gift can be done creatively and really add a lot of fun to gift-giving!

- ANGIE MEW
(HONOLULU, HAWAII)

KIDS FOR KIDS

Here's a great holiday idea! This is fun for one child to give to another. Buy clear craft ornaments (try Michaels craft store) and let them fill with whatever items they choose like glue, glitter, colored rice, dried flower petals or whatever their imagination comes up with, for a fun holiday gift. Another great twist is to cut up a one dollar bill in tiny fine pieces and put it inside the clear ornament. The kids won't believe they are cutting up money and the recipient will be thrilled with their money-filled ornament!

I love gifts that people make and some of my most favorite gifts are from kids - things that they make themselves. One example is as a picture of the child him or herself, with a home-made frame made out of toothpicks, string and shells. They put a backing on it and magnetic strips - this way I was able to put it on my fridge.

- CHRISTI NARRON
(KNIGHTDALE, NORTH CAROLINA)

DOLLAR STORE BUYS

If you have a dollar store located by you, go to it! You would be surprised at all the great finds that are there, from toys to elegant candles. You may not want to give these items as a gift alone, but you can find bits and pieces to add to your gift idea for only a dollar. Some of the great finds you will see include gift wrapping, candles, men's tool items, kitchen items, kids and baby toys, etc.

My aunt and godmother gave my daughter a handmade doll on her first Christmas.

The doll was hand-sewn with material taken from the clothing of family members! The skirt used material from my husband's favorite tee-shirt; the apron was made from my favorite lace shirt; bows in her hair were from my father's ascot; the pockets were from my grandmother's blouse; the brush in her pocket was my grandfather's.

She also put material from my daughter's sleeper on the doll. Her godparents had something belonging to them sewn onto the doll's dress. The list goes on and on! My aunt included card telling my daughter the story of what her dolly was made out of. One of her eyes might be smaller than the other, and her clothes might not match, but it is the most beautiful doll I have ever seen; and I know that the doll was stitched with love.

Maybe someday my daughter will sew a button on, put a ribbon in her hair or a hanky in her pocket and pass it on to her little girl.

- KRISTA HINCHEY
(GANDER, NEWFOUNDLAND)

BATHROOM FUN

Purchase a solid color plastic bathroom cup and paint a child's name on it with decorative and colorful paints. Add a toothbrush, toothpaste and floss. This gift is fun for the child and promotes good healthy teeth cleaning!

I have used coupons for years with my kids, which they love. I believe the gift of time is special. I started using coupons when my kids were small and I was a single parent with very little money. I always put it in their Christmas stockings. Examples of coupon gifts for kids are:

- *Dinner of choice*
- *Favorite dessert*
- *Car ride some place*
- *Staying up an hour past bedtime*
- *Extra batteries for toys*
- *Room cleaning*
- *Chores for a day or a week*
- *A hug and a kiss for special times*
- *A camp out in the living room*
- *A friend staying over*
- *Good for one movie rental*

I did this till they were in their teens and then I thought they were too old, so one year I didn't do it. They were very disappointed! By New Year's Day, they had their coupon books. When they were grown, they started giving me coupon books!

This is a true gift expressing love and building memories for children to carry with them forever!

- BEA JACOBS (TAYLOR, MICHIGAN)

KID KITS

Take a gift bag and add the following items for fun kits. Don't forget to add a tag explaining what the kit is all about!

- Rock Painting – Paints, paintbrush, clean rocks & art smocks.
- Shoelace Art – White shoelaces & paints or markers.
- Scrapbook Kit – Package of paper, markers & stickers. Look for free idea flyers at your local craft store to add to your kit.
- Lemonade Stand – Yellow tablecloth, cups, lemonade and a sign.
- School Supplies – Pencils, pencil holder, paper, eraser, and a cool binder.
- Tub Time– They have to do it, so let's make it fun with bubbles, battery-operated water toys, tub paints, sponges or soaps.

For an inexpensive birthday gift, give a Beanie Baby with the same birth date as the recipient. Check the tag or check a Beanie Baby book for the date you have in mind.

- WENDY WOODS
(BELLEVUE, WASHINGTON)

MAKE-UP LESSON

Many young teenaged girls would grab the chance to have a professional show them how to put on make-up! Check with your hair stylist for recommendations of professionals in your area. Many will give the lesson for free with a purchase. This is a great way to build up a teen's confidence and a terrific help to her parents. Sometimes teens think they have to put on a lot to get noticed. Teach them that it is the opposite!

The best gift that I have made and love to give is a gift for a baby. I make plastic canvas blocks with jingle bells inside for happy noises. I also use the same blocks to make a hanging mobile for the nursery.
- KATHI BRADY
(CRANBERRY TWP. PENNSYLVANIA)

SHOWER RADIOS ARE A GREAT GIFT FOR TEENS.

FANNY PACK

Kids love these! Buy a plain one for a few dollars and paint their names on it with cloth paint. Add a few items or trinkets if desired. Give these out before a trip, and fill them with chap stick, sunglasses, disposable camera or cash.

When I was a nanny sometime ago, the children I cared for had $5.00 for a gift for the mom and dad at Christmas time. So we decided that we would get creative. First we got a large box (about the size of a 19-inch TV). Then we went to the grocery store and bought two packs of cocoa mix and some chocolate bars. The family had a fireplace but never used it; so we bought a small bunch of wood that the grocery store was selling, and we headed home. Once we got there, we made beautiful homemade Christmas cards and really thought about what we wanted to say in them. We wrapped the wood. Found two mugs in the cabinet and stuffed the cocoa mix inside. We then wrapped it all up in the large box. We decorated the box with leftover wrapping paper and ribbon.

Then Christmas morning came...Mom and Dad opened their box together and everyone cheered while they pulled all the "goodies" out of the box. The parents were absolutely touched by the planning and the idea of giving a memory. Since that time I have carried that tradition forward with other "memory" moments with my family. All in all I'm not sure who had the most fun, the kids, myself or the parents.

- CATHY FUNDERBURG
(APOLLO BEACH, FLORIDA)

TEEN LOCKER FUN

Give a small corkboard with creative and unique push pins so they can hang their pictures and notes in their locker, in style! You can also make and decorate small mirrors with Velcro backing to stick inside the locker, or add Velcro to items like lip gloss, chap stick, combs or brushes.

Teenagers love cash, so here is an easy gift, adding a little charm for the holidays. Make a stuffed snowman, and tie a $10.00 bill around the neck as the scarf. Take a regular men's tube sock and stuff the bottom third with stuffing or cotton. Tie tightly with thread. Then do the middle of the body the same with a little less stuffing and tie with thread. Then do the top. Sew on eyes, nose, whatever you want and wrap the bill around the neck. It is less than $2.00 to make each snowman and nicer than just giving them money.

- CATHERINE DONELAN
(STONY POINT, NEW YORK)

HIGH SCHOOL & COLLEGE STUDENTS

There is nothing better for these kids than cash, but here are a few other ways to give it without handing out impersonal bills.

* Gas Card
* Phone Card
* Cell Phone Card
* Movie Certificates
* McDonalds Certificates
* Fit Food Pack - Pack a box or bag full of granola bars, fruit snacks, carnation instant breakfast and instant soups!
* Bathroom Supplies - hair items, lotions, soaps, personal hygiene items. We all need them!

Dreamcatchers can be a great gift idea for people of any age. They are meant to watch over us as we sleep. A child will hang their dreamcatcher by their bed and treasure it for years. For people that are ill, being given a dreamcatcher to get well, will have them so all their worries go away because they will know they are being watched over. They come in different sizes and colors and will be cherished for years to come.

- CASSANDRA NORTON
(MALONE, NEW YORK)

LIGHTS ON

Decorate a light bulb with glass paint for beautiful colored lighting. Add swirls and designs to make a great gift for all ages. A Girl Scout troop made these for a gift exchange, putting them in clear cellophane bags and wrapping them in ribbon. They were grabbed up immediately!

My grandchildren are between ages five and nine, so I try to come up with ideas for gifts that will keep them busy and instill creativity. One of my favorites is to make a set of bean bag throws by making a small square or round cloth bag and filling it with rice, sewing the end closed. They will toss them around for hours. For special wrapping, I put the bean bags in a tote bag that I make and then they also have something to keep them in.

- GLORIA MCMICAN
(FLORENCE, KENTUCKY)

PERSONALIZED GYM CLOTHES

Many sporting goods shops offer silk screening. Add the kids' names to a pair of shorts or to the back of a shirt for gym class. It usually costs about fifty cents a letter. It will also help keep track of those gym clothes since their name is on the back; if lost, they usually get returned.

When I went to Morocco to stay with my mother-in-law, I walked along the streets seeing mothers with babies putting their hands out for loose change to pay for medical bills. Every day that I was there I gave my loose change to those less well-off than me. Children were on the street selling a variety of things like home made bracelets, crisps, fizzy drinks to bring home money to their families for food. They were not allowed home until they made enough money. Every time I saw these children in the street I would buy as many bracelets as I could. I gave them to my children so they could give them to friends back home and explain why they were purchased and how lucky we are to have what we have. Children make wonderful gifts and our support not only helps them in different ways but it also helps ourselves.

-YVONNE WILTSHIRE
(CHARMOUTH, DORSET, ENGLAND)

DAY WITH FRIENDS

Plan an event for a few hours or a day with the child and two friends. Let them plan it by giving them the ideas. Here are a few sets you can give to start their planning:

* Swim Fun - Swim goggles, water bottles, water toys and sunscreen.
* Park Picnic - Box filled with a Frisbee, cups, 2 liter of soda, snacks and outdoor games.
* Library Fun - A nice quiet event that kids seem to love! Grab the library cards, maybe a sack lunch for a break.

Although these gifts may seem like everyday things that you do, they aren't - because you are allowing the child to plan their own event, which makes them feel special. A great deal for under $10.00!

This is a gift that was received by my son for his first birthday. My parents had to give up their home in New York and move to Ohio shortly after my son was born due to the closing of the Republic Steel Corp. where my father worked. For my son's first birthday, my mom sent him a letter for his journal. I'm sure she never realized how important it would turn out to be. You see, my son was only three when she died prematurely at age 48. So he had no real memories of her other than through pictures, and things our family has told him about her. The only direct link to her is the letter she sent him. My son is 24 now and to me this gift is priceless.
- NANCY BRIDENBAKER (ANGOLA, NEW YORK)

Chapter Three: Baby Gifts & Gifts For New Moms

If you've been shopping in baby stores lately, you know how expensive these family additions can be! How can you celebrate Junior's arrival in a way that Mom and Dad will remember, and thank you for – without spending your entire paycheck?

Here are some terrific ways to say you care about both Baby and his or her new family!

BABY BLANKET

Purchase enough fleece material at the fabric store for the size blanket you would like to make. Cut the edges in strips 2" up and 1" apart all along the edge of the blanket. Tie each piece next to each other in a knot - it's that simple! A darling, super soft blanket that baby will love!

Once, I gave my best friend a sentimental card; but instead of just giving the card, I framed it. It has been enjoyed for years. You can do with same thing, making framed art for baby's room.

- DEB SOLBERG
(PHOENIX, ARIZONA)

Knights of the Round Table Talk - Whenever we had this, we used a talking feather, which was a feather that was passed from one to another; when you had the feather you had the floor and everyone had to listen. This was safe time when you could let out either happy things or anger things and you were allowed to let the feelings out safely with no parent saying "I don't want to hear that" when the child is talking.

- BEA JACOBS
(TAYLOR, MICHIGAN)

PHOTOS ON THE GO

Take a roll of pictures of baby and put them in a small flip album that Mom can take along in her purse as a special brag book. In the first page, slip in a piece of paper with babies name, date of birth, weight, parents names, etc.

My craft-y sister-in-law made me a photo album on which she'd scanned and enlarged - and printed on fabric - a picture of me when I was five, next to a picture of my daughter at the same age. Pretty amazing!

- KATE FALVEY
(LONG BEACH, NEW YORK)

PERSONALIZED PENCILS ARE A BIG HIT! THE LILLIAN VERNON CATALOG OFFERS A VARIETY OF THEM.

29

BLANKET BASKET

Wrap needed baby items like washcloths, diapers, formula, toys, and bottles in the center of a receiving blanket. Pull the sides up and secure with a large 2" wired ribbon. It will be a fun surprise to open.

The Hallmark stores carry a red plate, with the words inscribed around the border (in white), "You are Special Today." While raising five children, my husband and I found it difficult to set aside quality time with one child, who may have achieved quite an accomplishment that should have been recognized by the entire family. Whether it be a fantastic improvement on a report card, the earning of a special badge through Scouts, or a sports championship win - whatever the special occasion may have been. When we set the dinner table (the one meal we always seemed to eat together as a family), the child being recognized would eat off the red plate. It truly was an honor for the special child! Everyone would ask questions about the event we were celebrating, give them a round of applause, and ask them to tell all the details during that specific dinner-time. The plate came with a black marker pen, so the name, date and event could be recorded on the back of the plate. This was over 30 years ago and I still see these plates in the Hallmark stores. I have already passed the plate down to the next generation. The designated person was a child with the most recognized events. He has kept it in a glass cabinet for the other siblings to see; and they seem to share these memories at yearly family events. It has been a highlight of shared moments.

- DARLA AGTARAP
(HELENA, MONTANA)

MOM'S HELPER SERVICE

A service of any kind is a great help to a new mom! Check pricing for a one-time diaper service visit, nanny service, or house cleaning; or donate your time to mom for babysitting so she can have a night out!

A very memorable gift for children is a hands-on project you do while they are young and give to them when they are older. Purchase an old wooden table at a garage sale, or small end tables for multiple children, something of this nature. Sand the top of the table so it is bare and let the children add pictures, writings etc. Finish with decoupage or a thick clear sealer for the top. These tables will be loved throughout their growing years and when they are older they will treasure them as well.

- LINDA RAYNOVIC
(DEWEY, ARIZONA)

FRAMED MONEY

Purchase a one-dollar bill and coins that are dated the same date as the year of the birth of baby. You can use matting and cut out a circle to stick the coins in and lay the dollar flat, lining up the dollar on the top and coins underneath. A special keepsake!

I received a framed collage of helpful baby tips, signed by everyone who attended my son's baby shower. Each person wrote a helpful hint or a short poem or nursery rhyme on a colored index card and signed it. The shower coordinator then glued these cards to a poster board she'd matted and framed (with materials bought at a discount craft shop for around $10). Not only was it a really cute decoration for my son's room, but some of the tips really came in handy, such as where to buy or how to make certain items cheaply, tips on treating diaper rash, colic, teething pain, temper tantrums, etc.
-TONYA JOHNSON
(ROCKY HILL, KENTUCKY)

LIGHT UP THEIR NIGHT

Sometimes babies need a nightlight all the way through their junior years. Unique nightlights can be found in many stores and will be much appreciated. You can even buy a clear-faced front one and decorate or add their name to it.

Make an ink print of a child hand or foot and put it on a regular piece of paper (or for better effect, some parchment paper) with the child's name and the date or occasion of the gift printed on the paper. Then frame it in an inexpensive frame (simple wood ones work best). This is good for a first Christmas, Mother's and Father's Days, and birthdays. This is also good for grandparents or out of town relatives. Unless you buy special paper, or have to buy an inkpad, this gift is only the cost of the frame, which I usually get for between two and five dollars.

- TIFFANY CLEMMONS
(POWHATAN, VIRGINIA)

BABY TEETH KEEPSAKE

Give a handmade or store-bought baby teeth box. After the tooth fairy comes, Mom can put away the teeth in this box. This will be another keepsake that is around for a long time!

For a cute gift idea that helps muscle pain, relieves stress, or just plain soothes you, try a handmade "rice sock." Take a men's large size long white tube sock and fill it with plain white rice. Leave enough room on both ends to tie it off with pretty ribbon (strips of colorful cloth work well too). You should then have a long, soft, slender shaped wrap. You can further decorate it by drawing or sewing a person's name on it or drawing flowers, etc... When you are ready to use, just pop it into the microwave for a minute or two and it will warm up the rice. The rice sock will stay warm for quite a while and you can wrap it around your tired neck, your sore lower back or really any body part that needs a warm-up!
- KERRI FREUNDSCHUH
(ALBANY GEORGIA)

VIDEO/DVD

Babies and kids love videos, so get them one for the future that they will play over and over. Musicals, educational and classics are among children's favorites. If you want to take a little time building a small library for them, watch your garage sales for newer videos and add them to a basket. If you can pick them up for $1.00 each, you could have a basket of fun for $10.00! Great kid entertainment for Mom, too!

When my children were young, you would always find a string of wishbones hanging in my kitchen. I never let anyone break them and I told the kids we needed to let them dry by hanging them up. What I was really doing was saving them for the right moment. Whenever someone was going through a tough time, was sad, or just really needed to make a wish, then they were allowed to pick a wish bone. It is a simple idea and it was a fun gift from Mom to the kids.

- LINDA RAYNOVIC
(DEWEY, ARIZONA)

CHAPTER FOUR: CO-WORKER GIFTS

We've probably all had it happen at one time or another - been overwhelmed with a project or responsibility, and then had someone, out of the blue, appear to help us with it. How do you thank your guardian angel for his or her help?

And then there are the birthdays, the promotions, the person who always gets coffee on Fridays... the list of occasions goes on and on, but your creativity might be faltering by now. What exactly do you give to a co-worker?

In the next pages, we'll answer all those dilemmas. The key is to think - as the jargon would have it - outside the box. Read on and discover the limitless gift-giving options for the workplace!

BREAKFAST TREAT

Bring your co-worker a latte, bagel, smoothie, bowl of fruit or yogurt. A great way to start their special day!

At Christmas time, I fill cellophane bags with my grandmother's recipe of homemade fudge and cookies. I add a printed copy of the recipe on a small card, attaching it to the bags with ribbon. Friends and family members can use the recipe throughout the year.
- LUCY LEON
(LA PUENTE, CALIFORNIA)

Remind yourself when you are searching for a gift that it is your intention to make someone happy or feel special. Forget about what everyone else is giving and really think about what your recipient would enjoy and appreciate. Give what you think that person would want - not what you would want in their place.

THE SNACK PACK

Junk food is always a big hit at the office - or, for that matter, at any job! Fill any kind of container with chips, candy bars, boxed juices and fun snacks that are out of the ordinary. Even a brown lunch sack with someone's name on it in big letters is a fun surprise!

As a business owner, I am often trying to think of little ways to say thank you to my customers. This gift idea has been a big hit! I use small koosh jungle animals in bright colors that I purchase from a party store for about 30 cents each. I then wrap them in a small cellophane bag and add a fluorescent label. I write THANKS on the label - and have received many thanks in return from my customers for the tiny gift!
- MOUNTAIN VIEW HYPNOTHERAPY
(LYNNWOOD, WASHINGTON)

DO THEIR JOB

Give a certificate entitling them to pass one of their duties to you. Not a project that requires their own expertise, but something simple such as filing, or some other chore that they just don't seem to want to get done. You may need to check with your boss on this one, or consider using a half-hour of your lunch break to do the task.

Here is a big hit for the co-workers! I take a small candy jar with a lid. Purchase a small stuffed animal, preferably one in a sitting position, and separate the head from the body (I know it sounds cruel) but it is very cute! Remove the stuffing from the head, apply hot glue to the inside of the head and place over the jar lid. Then, take the legs (leave stuffing in) and glue one leg to each side of the jar. If there is a tail you can glue the tail to the back of the jar. Then fill the jar with candy or goodies to give as a gift.

- KATHY OAKES
(NORWOOD, NEW YORK)

OFFICE SUPPLIES

How about a funky pen, a stylish notepad, or sticky notes? Almost everyone uses pens in their line of work and many department stores now carry unique gift pens for as low at $6.00. Try ebay for creative office tools.

Give a box of the best pastries in town! A rich delicacy full of chocolate, cream and all the sweet things they add. What a treat and a great gift for many reasons under $10.00!

- NANCY MALTAIS
(GILMANTON IRONWORKS, NEW HAMPSHIRE)

STRESS BALLS ARE HANDY TO RELIEVE ON-THE-JOB FRUSTRATIONS, IN A SILENT WAY!

CALENDAR

We use them at home, we use them at work. Calendars make great gifts and aren't thought of enough. Mini wall calendars are small and convenient for hanging on a bulletin board. Purchase magnet backs or suction hooks for hanging in creative places.

When my cousin graduated from high school, her older sister and I threw her a party and invited her closest friends. We had each friend come one hour early and bring a photo of them with my cousin. We then mounted the photos on an oversized poster board we'd matted and framed and had them add monologue stickers to each photo with a cute saying describing the picture. This collage of photos was presented as the grand finale of the party and to this day (it's been over 10 years) she still has that poster on the wall in her computer room and meets regularly with those friends for a "girl's night out." They have continued to add to the poster over the years and are about to start another one that will include their spouses and children.

- TONYA JOHNSON
(ROCKY HILL, KENTUCKY)

PERSONALIZE IT

Check with your local printer about printing notepads, letterhead, note cards and envelope with your co-worker's name on them. A set of plain note cards with initials on the front are often used for quick notes, thank you cards, etc. Current, Inc. also offers personalized items (see reference page). This is one of the gifts that most people will not buy for themselves.

One year, for Christmas, my gift to family and friends was a stationery set of 30 sheets, 10 envelopes, and 1 sheet of 30 address labels. I used my Printmaster program and made backgrounds using what I knew about the person (their favorite color, flower, hobby, etc.). Everyone really seemed to enjoy them, and it only cost the amount of a package of paper, boxes of envelopes, and packs of address labels for however many people you're making them for. You can adjust the quantity of items in each set to your own preferences.

- LORRI JONES
(FRESNO, CALIFORNIA)

CAR CADDY

Many people use their vehicle daily for business, as well as taking long trips. Consider something they often use in their car, such as tissues, a neck pillow, a cup holder, or perhaps a new CD. Small thin fleece blankets are super for extra comfort while driving and are available at many department stores for about $8.00.

A fun idea that I had done for sorority and other activities in the past has been to find a cheap decorative pot or oversized coffee cup (and a cut plastic container will also work). Add a little potting soil and a small plant, such as a spring of ivy, vine plant, jade or Christmas cactus that does not need roots to get going. Add decorative items to the container if you wish, and you have a quick yet simple gift for friends or as a get-well gesture. It gives people in the hospital something to take home and remember the donor.

- JANESSA BUTTERFIELD
(MARYVILLE, MISSOURI)

CHAPTER FIVE:
BRIDAL SHOWER AND
WEDDING GIFTS &
ROMANCE

Ah, romance... it just cries out for gifts to be "showered" on the new couple! But do you have to give crystal and china?

Not at all! Your gifts are limited only by your budget and your imagination, and in the next few pages, you'll find marvelous, romantic, even passionate gifts that will delight anyone in love... and at a fraction of what you thought you'd spend!

Making gifts personal is the key. Romance is nothing if not personal, and so too should be your gifts!

GREENERY

A plant! So simple and with so much meaning! Plants will last for years when taken care of. Every time the recipient looks at them, he or she will think of the gift-giver. If you aren't sure what type of plant to give, go to your local nursery and ask for a hearty indoor plant under $10.00. You'll be surprised at the variety. Now that is value!

About sixteen years ago, I was having a bad time and wanted to feel that I had some success in life. I use the word "win" to describe a goal that I've gone after and have reached. I was complaining to my then husband how I needed to have some wins! I was so terribly frustrated and depressed. Later that day, he handed me a shoebox and told me to open it. My mood instantly shifted from despair to delight when I opened the box. Inside, on at least fifty small pieces of paper, he had written the word "win." I needed some "wins" and he gave me an entire box full of them!

- HEIDI THOMPSON
(LAS VEGAS, NEVADA)

ENTERTAINING FUN

Many newlyweds don't have necessary items for entertaining guests. Consider a book on entertaining, a set of wine stoppers, a wine chiller, an appetizer cookbook or a serving tray for chips and salsa.

In the first couple of years after I was married I would often call my mom, frantic.

"Mom, how do you make Glorified Brownies?"

"Mom, how do you make gravy?"

"Mom, how do you make your spaghetti sauce?"

Well, I think my Mom was sick of all the phone calls! The best gift I received was one Christmas when she made me the "Grebe Family Cookbook." They weren't all Mom's recipes. Some were from family friends. There was even a whole section on cooking a turkey, and making all the other Thanksgiving fixin's. She also sprinkled little quotes about life lessons through the years.

Everything was just printed from a computer. The book she bought for the recipes is nice, but I would love this book even if it were just stapled together! My mom also purchased dividers (1, 2, 3, 4...) to make chapters. I don't think it was a very expensive gift, but it was rich in time and love! It was the best present I have ever received from her. Not only is it great to have lots of childhood recipes, but Mom also included the stories behind them. Those stories are like little treasures that I cherish every time I open the book. I use this book all the time and I constantly bug her for Volume Two! What about goulash and corn fritters? It's amazing how many recipes we still come up with.

- TRICIA SCHMITZ
(MENASHA, WISCONSIN)

GIVING A SHOWER?

A great gift for guests is to take a champagne or wine glass (you can pick up brand new ones at second hand stores for as low as 25 cents) and fill it with candy. Take a 5"x 11" cellophane bag and set the cup inside, tying the top with ribbon. Add a small gift tag to the ribbon that reads, "It was sweet of you to think of me." Or, "You're worth a mint." Come up with your own personalized saying. This idea is also a big hit in the business world as a small thank-you for clients.

As a little favor for the bride to be, I buy packs of "Sniffs," which are essentially decorative tissues. I take a couple of tissues and seal them in cellophane bags to be handed out with programs at the church. Seal the cellophane bag with a heat seal or ribbon. Very cute, very cheap and a nice little wedding extra.

- TRACEY SHARIS
(BOSTON, MASSACHUSETTS)

FAVORITE RECIPES

Finding a good recipe always takes time. Take a few of your favorites, and maybe someone else's, and put them in a small 3"x 5" photo album for easy access and storage. We always seem to want to try a new recipe that someone has recommended.

My husband once wrote me a poem and then had a friend make the poem into an iron-on transfer, which is easy to do with a computer and printer, using special paper. Then he had the poem ironed onto a sweatshirt for me to wear. The only real cost was the sweatshirt.
- KIMBERLY VETRANO
(POMONA, NEW YORK)

MATCHING HIS/HER SLIPPERS IS A GIFT THAT WILL BE RECEIVED WITH SMILES AT A BRIDAL SHOWER.

PHOTO CERTIFICATE

Give someone a certificate for a set of photo reprints or enlargements. Another approach is to call your local photo studio and ask about creative ideas that they have to make a memorable photo gift.

My husband gave me the best gift ever on my 35th birthday. We didn't have a lot of extra money, and he probably spent a total of $20.00 for everything, but it was HUGE! Using pink curling ribbon, he tied a balloon and a small gift (a pack of stick pins). About every three feet or so, there was another balloon. There were about 10 little $.50 cent sewing-related gifts attached at the bottom of every third balloon. There are 35 balloons on this tremendously long string of balloons that stretched out about 100 feet. I sat on the couch, and he asked me to "pull" my birthday present in. My husband did this with the help of my then four-year-old son, who loved it! It was the most thoughtful gift my husband has ever given me. I had so much fun, and so did he in orchestrating the travel of the balloon train through the house to allow me to pull it into the living room. Once the gifts were removed, I pulled all the strings together and with some cutting and arranging, I had a really nice, colorful and big balloon bouquet. My husband chose colors that I love and he put so much thought into it that I can't ever imagine anything topping that one. Creative and thoughtful!

- TINA WISELY
(INDIANAPOLIS, INDIANA)

Stock-Up Box For Newlyweds

This is so much fun, and a gift I have given many times!
Wrap a box with wedding gift-wrap in such a way that
the lid opens. Include tons of items that all newlyweds
might need. Here is a list of items - and yes, you can do
this for $10.00!

Toothpicks	Spoon Holder
Kitchen Sponges	Napkin Holder
Kitchen Soap	Kitchen Timer
Cleaners	Mini Serving Spatula
Mini Utensils	Hand Shredder
Gravy Packets	Garlic Press
Spatulas	Measuring Spoons
Dish Rags	Plant Food
Soup Mixes	Hot Pad/ Oven Mitt
Wine Opener	Air Fresheners
Napkins/Paper towels	Candles
Baggies	Address Book/Pen

Sometimes it is the simple things that are so much fun!

---

*Something as simple as an elegant single rose will surely
make someone's day!*
                    *- KRISTIN PRESTHOLDT JOHNSHOY
                        (DAWSON, MINNESOTA)*

ICE CREAM FIXIN'S

How about an unusual gift? Include all the yummy items to make ice cream sundaes or banana splits. Add it all to sundae bowls or banana split trays; even if they are plastic, the newlyweds will love it!

My fiancé and I are young and just getting started in life, which leaves us financially limited. So we really enjoy looking through thrift stores and used book stores together. It is an inexpensive way to indulge one of our favorite hobbies, shopping. We had stopped in one of our favorite little thrift shops one evening. I spotted a very nice Victorian themed piece of framed art entitled "Love Letters." It was priced at $10. I mentioned that I liked it, but it was more than I wanted to spend so I left without it. Then about a month later I came home from work and it was sitting on the couch for me. He had gone back that day and it was still there, so he bought it for me. I thought that was such a sweet gift. Not only did I like the picture, I was more touched that he remembered it so long afterward. It was a nice reminder of our special times together, which is better than an expensive present any day. Gifts from the heart!

*- JESSICA CHRISTENSEN
(GRESHAM, OREGON)*

INSPIRATIONAL CANDLE

Paste an inspirational poem or saying for the new couple on a wide pillar candle using decoupage, which is the art of cutting, assembling, and pasting paper cutouts. (If you want to learn more, there are lots of great books out there about decoupage. Try it - it's easy, fun, and inexpensive!) You can even use a thin picture, adding a memorable photo of their early times together.

Poem-photos are fun, inexpensive and meaningful. Take a photo and mount it on a large piece of paper. Write a funny message or sentimental poem about this person and add it to the paper with the picture, then frame. The ones I have made have been mounted on their wall with pride and they treasure them!

-MELISSA SAMATAS
(QUEBEC, CANADA)

HOMEOWNERS DIARY

It isn't elegant, but what a great organizer to have! A record book of all improvements and important information about the house, including appliances, etc. This is fun for a new couple to fill out together, and it is a great selling feature when they go to sell their house. Available at many bookstores and through Current, Inc.

Buy a pretty, shiny red key (I even saw fancy keys at Wal-Mart recently - leopard print, flowers, etc, which only cost $1.00 to $3.00). Put it in a pretty gift box and give it to your sweetie. When they open it they always ask "What does this go to?" and you reply "It's the key to my heart!" Ooooooooohhhhh - mushy, mushy!

Here is a similar idea, the difference being that you purchase some of those arts and craft "eyes" that move, and glue them onto the cotton in the gift box - wrap it prettily with a note that says, "I only have eyes for you!" This always gets a great response - I know, because my high school boyfriend gave this to me when I was 16 and I loved it! I thought he was the most clever and romantic guy in the world!

- JENNIFER PATTISON
(YORKTOWN, VIRGINIA)

EVENT TICKETS

Get the recipient tickets to an upcoming event, like a special theatre show or play. Try to get your tickets for months in advance. Another idea is to give them a schedule of events and a certificate toward one, so they can choose their own event. Many people have never been to a theatre show or play; and they provide hours of entertainment. This can be a very fulfilling evening for a new couple and it is always exciting to try something new.

A simple romantic gift would be to fill a hatbox with two wine glasses, coupons for massages by partner, chocolate or chocolate-dipped strawberries, etc."
- AZANA JOHNSON
(ROSEVILLE, CALIFORNIA)

CHAPTER SIX
THE LOVELY LADY RELATIVES IN YOUR LIFE

They say that women are easy to buy for; but that's not always the case. After all, how many bottles of perfume can one girl use?

Give these lovely ladies what they deserve: something that was thought of with them, uniquely, in mind. Give them gifts that will keep them smiling and remembering you for longer than that bottle of perfume would have lasted!

THE BAKER

Take a clear plastic bag and add fun bakery items, tying with a colorful ribbon at the top. Consider adding a new recipe, blank recipe cards, cookie cutters, a cookbook, baking utensils, sprinkles, chocolate chips, etc.

A friend who moved away left me a gift to open a week after their departure. It was very memorable for me! It was a tea bag with a little card that read, "The miles might divide us, but together we will be, so go & put the kettle on and have a cup of tea. I'll be thinking of you as you think of me." We shared many conversations over a 'brew' and now each time I put the kettle on, I think of her.

- ANGE THOMPSON
(ENGLAND)

MEASURING CUP MIX

Instead of the mix in a jar, add ingredients in a clear bag and set it in a nice new glass measuring cup, tying the recipe to the cup handle. Add curling ribbon to the handle for abright and festive look.

A special gift that I have given is a set of personally-decorated journal books with pens, one for a friend and one for me. We then filled the books with thoughts, feelings, crafts, and pictures until they were full, and then we exchanged them. We are delighted in each other's gift. It also works really well to use with teenagers who are timid to talk but more open to written thoughts.
- TASSIE DIMMITT
(SAN MARCOS, CALIFORNIA)

OVEN MITT TREAT

Everyone could use an extra or new oven mitt around the kitchen. Add items like cocoa, marshmallows, candy etc. Add a gift card or note that reads, "I have to admitt, you are great!" Tie ribbon through the loop of the mitt, adding your special note. Roll up a few matching kitchen towels or washcloths to add inside. A small chocolate truffle costs about 25 cents and will brighten just about anyone's day. She'll always think of you when she uses her kitchen mitt.

When I was in the hospital, my sister-in-law brought me a basket full of coloring books, word finds, crossword puzzles, crayons, pens, pencils, and a deck of cards. She had found everything at a dollar store at four for $1.00. The whole gift was $8.00 and I thought it was wonderful, as it gave me something to do while I was stuck in bed all day.

- AMY ULIBARRI
(PHOENIX, ARIZONA)

PHOTOS

Try these fun ideas using photographs:

* Purchase peel-and-stick magnets at your local office supply store and add a photo for a fridge magnet.
* Add to coffee mug.
* Mouse pad photos are a great way to make someone smile while at the office!
* Use any calendar and cover the picture with a photo collage.
* Make your photo into a bookmark.

For housewarming presents, I usually bring potted plants ($0.99 to $1.99) from Target, coupled with plain ceramic pots and matching saucers ($0.99 - $3.99 from a crafts store like Michaels). If the recipient has children, all the better. I bring one plant and one pot and saucer for each of the hosts and their children. The craft store sells permanent marker pens made especially to decorate pottery. The pens aren't cheap, approximately $16.00 for a set of 6 colors, but I take them home with me. We decorate the pots together, each of us decorating a pot and saucer, then plant the plants in them. Wonderfully received!

- GREAT GIFT GIVER
(MENLO PARK, CALIFORNIA)

STATIONERY SET

Note cards are always nice; but take this gift one step further! Add a pen and some stamps so they are ready for writing and mailing. You may even add a pretty package of envelope sealers or stickers. Wrap with raffia ribbon around the set for an added festive touch. A very useful set of items she is sure to use.

I made calendars for my family one year. I went through some pictures that I had, and picked out the most memorable for each family that I was making a calendar for (my parents, my husband's parents, my brother's family, and so on). Then I scanned a picture, using the different options of borders, shading, and various extras. I entered a month for the coming year for each picture, then tied them all together with yarn. Everyone who received one was taken aback by the thought that went into the gift. Even though making a lot of calendars can really use up the printer ink, I believe that I managed to make six calendars for only the cost of my paper, which was $10.

- BETH LESHER
(NEWTON FALLS, OHIO)

LOAF SET

Add a five-star recipe and mix for a loaf of bread to a new loaf pan. Wrap a piece of wide ribbon lengthwise on the pan for an elegant look. This is an exciting gift that can be used right away or saved for a special time.

When I was a child in the mid 40s, the Christmas season was one you wouldn't forget! About two months before Christmas, my mother would start preparing plum pudding, as it had to age and was kept in the cellar where it was cold. We always knew when she was done with it as her wedding band disappeared. The reason for that is she wrapped it in wax paper and put it in the pudding along with other items. When everyone was served their pudding they would watch to see what everyone got! Here are some of the items and their meanings that we would find in the pudding:

- *Wedding ring - meant you would marry*
- *Dime - you would be rich*
- *Penny - you would be poor*
- *Button - you would be a bachelor*
- *Thimble - you would be an old maid*

She had about a dozen items total and a memory that will be with me forever!

- NORM WITHERBEE
(HELENA, MONTANA)

THE OLDER GENERATION

Many folks are on fixed income and living on a budget. You can do so many things just by giving them a card and add an idea here to help them lighten their load:

- Give a $10.00 Wal-Mart gift card.
- Send in a few bucks as a credit to their phone bill.
- Buy a geranium or potted flower for their porch.
- Pay for lawn service.
- Drop by with an extra bag of groceries.

My parents are retired and live on a fixed income. My mother's sister lived on the other side of the state, so phone calls were long distance and my mother limited her calls to keep the bill down. I decided to give her a phone card that I got very reasonably from Costco so she could talk whenever she wanted to and not have to worry.

It just so happened it came at a very good time. Her sister became quite ill and was in the hospital for a very long time. When she finally got home, my mom called her daily just to see how she was doing. She improved, then suddenly took a turn for the worse and passed away rather quickly.

My mom is so thankful she had that card because she talked to her sister daily for two weeks before her passing. She said they had some wonderful conversations which she wouldn't have been able to do because she would not have called her as often.

- CJ SHOUMAN
(KENT, WASHINGTON)

CHAPTER SEVEN: NEIGHBORS

We like them, we don't like them... we live with them. Neighbors know more about us, sometimes, than our closest friends. So how can we reward them for listening to our kids playing, hearing our arguments, watching us mow the lawn, rescuing our cat from their tree?

Showing that you care and appreciate your neighbors doesn't have to put you in the poorhouse! Follow the "recipes" on the next few pages and see how much they'll appreciate you for your thoughtfulness!

BAKE IT FRESH

A cake, cookies, bread or any other sweet treats are always a welcome gift. This is one of the nicest gestures because many members of the family can enjoy it and it will last a few days! In our fast-paced world it gets tough sometimes to bake for our family as we would like. This gift is appropriate year-round for birthdays, holidays or just because. Use a festive paper plate and wrap your items on the plate with saran wrap. Add a gift tag that reads, "Baked fresh for you, from me."

Attach the following message to the filled bucket:

This little "Love Bucket" is meant to express love from
a neighbor whom you'll never guess.
Replace the goodies with a treat from you.
And pass it on to someone whom you love too.

Once the buckets are ready, place them on the doorstep of your neighbor or friend, and run!

- ALISON RICHMOND
(WEST YORKSHIRE, UK)

JUST POPPED IN

Add the following to a gift bag: a two-liter bottle of soda, package of popcorn, M&Ms, and a $5.00 movie certificate. Attach a tag that reads, "Just Popping In To Say Hi!" Give as a holiday gift by adding the word "Holiday" before "Hi".

For an older person who loves the outdoors, I sent a donation to the Arbor Day Foundation on her behalf, with the acknowledgement card to be sent to her; I asked that they include a card from me. In the card I wrote, "I appreciate you as much as you appreciate trees and the outdoors."

She told me it was one of the best gifts she had ever received.

- LISA JEWETT
(FREDERICKSBURG, VIRGINIA)

GARDENER'S DREAM

Give the a helping hand in their garden by putting garden tools, kneepads and seeds in a planter box, pot or watering can.

My grandma was an amazing cook, and it was at her side that I learned much of what I know. Wherever she went she was always giving people something from her kitchen.

Chocolate-Covered Oreos
Use one large package of Oreo Cookies
12 - 16 oz semi-sweet chocolate coating or chocolate bits, plus one tablespoon shortening (helps coat smoothly).
2 oz white chocolate coating (optional)

Melt chocolate coating in a double boiler or microwave oven until smooth. Using a fork, dip cookies one at a time in the chocolate and gently shake off the excess. Place on wax paper or parchment paper. Let sit until chocolate has hardened.

(Optional) Melt the white chocolate and us a fork to drizzle it over the cookies to create a decorative pattern and let harden.

Makes approximately 36 cookies. Experiment with different varieties of Oreos, like mint, or use different kinds of chocolate to coat. You can even use white chocolate for coating, and tint it with food color for holidays. I used mini Oreos coated in pastel-tinted white chocolate and drizzled a different pastel color over them for Easter.

- LARRY PFEIL (NEW YORK, NEW YORK)

TIDY UP

Mow a neighbor's lawn, trim the hedges and trees, or shovel the driveway if it has snowed. You can even pick up the leaves, which is always a great help. Make it a family affair having each member tackling one task. You will be done in no time flat and you'll feel great about it. Leave a small note at the door letting them know about your gift. Suggest that it's a good opportunity for them to rest and relax!

For a birthday gift, give the child $1 for every year that child is old. Increase the gift $1 annually every remaining birthday - even as the child becomes an adult. A child has to become quite old for this gift to become expensive.

- HEIDE SALTER
(YPSILANTI, MICHIGAN)

DÉCOR

Give a new doorbell ringer, garden ornament, updated house numbers or mailbox numbers. Make sure you let them know that this is not meant as an insult but a fun home update!

Years ago, I was visiting one of my younger sisters, who is very creative. She made very small homemade Christmas ornaments and gave me a few. They had incredible detail, with small beads and lace edging, and she used white cotton snow. These are on the top of my treasured gifts list.

Ornaments are a creative gift for neighbors during the holidays!

- ANN TANNER
(NEWPORT BEACH, CALIFORNIA)

CHAPTER EIGHT: ALL THOSE TOUGH-TO-BUY-FOR MALES

It is a fact that men are just tougher to buy for. The thought in giving is what counts, so let's not make this so tough on ourselves! One thing most men love to do is eat, so let's see what we've got...

OFFICE TREATS

If he works in an office, give him something he'll surely use, by filling a pen/pencil holder with items such as nuts, jerky, beef sticks etc. He can use the pencil holder afterward!

Last Christmas I bought three books with short stories from a library sale. I then read them onto tapes and gave them for gifts. I read some Shakespeare for my daughter and Reader's Digest short stories for my husband, as well as a devotional book with Bible scriptures.

I once read a children's book for a dear little friend with an assortment of kid's songs in the background.

I had a friend at the nursing home who liked mysteries but could no longer read, so I filled three tapes for him with what he liked. This is a gift that is inexpensive but filled with love and meaning!

--TASSIE DIMMITT
(SAN MARCOS, CALIFORNIA)

CAR WASH

Give a token for a car wash attached to a bottle of Armor All and a towel. Consider a certificate for a car wash by you! Another idea would be to surprise him with a car wash and wax by you, which costs very little, only your time. Men love their cars!

I like to give appropriate gift cards. I know it is not very original, but it's extremely practical. My favorite is Starbucks. You always know who likes Starbucks coffee, because they probably walk around with a Starbucks cup every morning when you see them. Well, we all know that coffee is not as cheap as it used to be, and many people would really enjoy receiving a $5.00 or $10.00 Starbucks Card. The great thing about it is that you can give it for any reason or for any occasion.

*- EVAN KRICHMAN
(LOS ANGELES, CALIFORNIA)*

Personalize It

Add name or initials to a pen, money clip, insulated travel mug, hat, jacket, or a coffee cup. Another great personalized gift is to take a T-shirt or work shirt and have his name embroidered on the pocket.

If a loved one is away from home, try a "scented pillow." When my husband was overseas for a long period of time in the military, I took a white pillowcase and used iron-on transfers to decorate the case. You could iron on designs or even a photo of yourself or your family. You can also use paints or other permanent markers to write messages on the pillowcase, such as "sweet dreams" or "sleep tight, don't let the bedbugs bite!" When you are finished decorating the pillowcase, spray it down with your favorite perfume or cologne and fold it up and store in an airtight Ziploc bag. I mailed one scented with my perfume to my husband all the way to Japan. The smell not only made it all the way there but it lasted for a couple of weeks until he finally had to wash the case! There is nothing like the smell of home!

- KERRI FREUNDSCHUH
(ALBANY, GEORGIA)

LOTTO

Scratch tickets are a fun item among men! Simply purchase a variety of 10 tickets for $1.00 each and add them to a greeting card. This is a favorite on many gift-giving lists.

The most special thing I ever bought someone was for my brother-in-law. He is a Civil War buff and over the years he has received books, movies, pc games, virtual tours, etc. I wanted something different so I used ebay. I found someone selling actual (and I think it really was actual) battlefield items. As I understand it, this person lives near many battle sites. He digs in certain areas and unearth items such as pieces of bullets and guns, uniforms, buttons, etc. These are not museum quality pieces, but authentic just the same.

I was able to get a 20-piece lot of all kinds of fragments for around $15.00. I then searched for weathered shadowboxes. I believe it cost 5.00 with shipping and handling. I got a sheet of self stick black felt and lined the shadowbox, added self-stick Velcro pieces, some pictures I downloaded from a Civil War site and made a display collection.

I am not a handy person but I gave my brother-in-law a one-of -a-kind treasure and he was in awe when he opened it. He had tears in his eyes and wonder in his voice. He cherishes this collection and it was WELL worth my time and effort. He still cannot get over that he has ACTUAL civil war items in his own home.

- KATHY DAVENPORT
(BALTIMORE, MARYLAND)

READY, SET, READ

Roll a new magazine or an out-of-state newspaper up in ribbon for entertaining reading. This is easy when you are traveling: just stop by a local convenience store or grab one if you are in an airport. If you would like to promote rest and relaxation for your hardworking man, add some jerky snacks to the rolled-up newspaper or magazines and include a homemade sign that reads:"This hardworking man is on break, do not disturb!"

As a grandpa who lives long distance from his grandkids; the most memorable gifts I have received are the pictures my daughter sends to me of my grandchildren. They are already framed, treasured and last forever.

- DENNIS FOURNIER
(PORT AUSTIN, MICHIGAN)

MONEY CAN

Decorate a coffee can with something of interest that they may like to save for – such as skiing, a sports event or a travel goal. Cut a slit in the top for their special savings money bank.

Print a description of the idea from your computer and tape it to your gift can—his own, personal savings plan. For kicks you could add a few coins to get him started. This is a great project gift for kids to make, also.

My boyfriend and I just celebrated our three-year anniversary, and I really struggled to think of something special to get for him or do for him. After much deliberation, while I was driving to work and singing along to a really sweet love song that always makes me smile and think of him, it came to me.

I decided to videotape myself singing this song to him for our anniversary.

It was sort of tricky to do on my own, but it turned out great, and he was moved almost to tears. No one had ever sung to him in his life. The total cost is $2.49 for the tape and a little time! He will always have my little rendition of a special love song to remember that day.

- BRENDA WORCESTER
(SOUTH PORTLAND, MAINE)

EXTRA SPECIAL YUMMIES

I've never known a man who didn't like cinnamon rolls or peanut brittle! Check out your local bakeries and dig around for homemade special yummies. Make them yourself or pick some up, adding a gift card and wrapping in a neutral color ribbon or raffia for a masculine look.

Fun-filled boxes make great gifts! If it's for a man, then purchase small bottles of cologne, some aftershave, deodorant, razors, playing cards, golf balls, hankies, writing pens etc., depending on the individual's interests or type of job. With women, it can be perfumes, lotions, bath oils, or items specific to their preferences. Maybe the person likes crafts. You could do a related gift box full of craft paints or brushes, knitting needles and yarn or patterns. The ideas for this type of gift are limitless and can be inexpensive if the items are purchased at a discount store. Kids are easy! I have many nieces and nephews and I usually do a box for both birthdays and Christmas. It will usually include some candies, balloons, cap guns or dolls and a bunch of those toys like cars, action figures, jump-ropes - you name it! These items are usually a dollar or less apiece and the kids love having such a wide variety to play with. The box itself doesn't matter. Any kind of box will work. Kids don't really care about the box nor do they appreciate fancy wrapping or bows. Good adult boxes are ones with lids. That way, both the box and the lid can be individually wrapped to make even a shoebox into a very nice gift box that is easy to open because all they have to do is take the string or ribbon off and lift the lid. Tissue paper can be added to lessen any rattles or used to layer items so they are seen one item at a time.
- STEVE HICKMAN (SPRINGFIELD, OHIO)

COMPUTER STOCK UP

Computer disks, mouse pad, magazines showing new products and programs available are great ideas for the computer nut! How-to books about a subject they have expressed an interest in learning are another great idea!

Here are a couple more:
- Batteries for a wireless mouse
- Pressurized can of air for cleaning
- Screen cleaner
- Jewel cases for CDs
- CD holder
- Wrist pad

If your man loves sports, consider giving a sports card of your guy's favorite player. You can mat and frame them for a unique gift that they can display on their desk or at home. Check your local sports card store or search the Internet.

- ERIC BROWN
(MOIRA, NEW YORK)

PUZZLES & GADGETS

Put those smarts to the test with brain-teaser puzzles and puzzle books. They only cost a few dollars for hours of entertainment.

Here are a few sources for great on-line puzzle mania:

- Areyougame.com
- ebay.com
- seriouspuzzles.com

The photo scanning capabilities these days are terrific! Scan an old sentimental picture at home or at a local department store and put it in a picture frame for a great gift!

**- KRISTIN PRESTHOLDT JOHNSHOY
(DAWSON, MINNESOTA)**

BBQ SET

Update his outdoor cookware with utensils, sauces and all those items men use. Top it off with a personalized apron for the BBQ master. Wrap all the special barbecue items up in the apron, tying it with a ribbon. No wrapping paper is necessary for this gift!

People generally love getting gifts from me because the gift is truly made with them in mind. Gifts certainly don't need to be extravagant to impress! That is the main reason I love gift baskets! You can spend very little for a gift with pizzazz! Pick up baskets on clearance racks and use some of these ideas:

- *For a busy friend with small children, how about a little basket with some fruit, homemade cookies and those little fruit drink pouches? What a nice way to give your friend a little time away from "Mommy! I'm hungry!"*
- *For the executive type man, how about a travel pouch with pocket items like Aqua Velva deodorant wipes, some Spray and Wash individual wipes, Chap Stick, men's handkerchiefs, a small sewing kit and breath mints?*
- *For a sick child, you can purchase a personal CD or tape player now for around $5. Add some Life Savers and a small cuddle toy and presto! Smiles guaranteed!*

- TRUDY SARATA
(ROCK HILL, SOUTH CAROLINA)

CAR STUFF

Fill a travel mug with an auto litter bag, car clock, air freshener, cleaners, wipes or whatever else he may use in his vehicle! If he travels frequently, a nice gift would be a quick car cleaning and vacuuming prior to his next trip.

I can say that one of the BEST gifts that I have received that was FREE and from the heart came from my husband, Robert, before we were even married. He took a glass bottle (something one might fill with colorful sand - like sand art) and broke up a small wooden ruler into tiny pieces and filled the bottle with the pieces. He then made a label for the bottle that read, "I broke up this ruler because it is impossible to measure my love for you." It was totally free and totally from the heart. I still have it and I keep it on my desk so I can look at it every day. This gift could be given to a man just as well.
- KIMBERLY VETRANO
(POMONA, NEW YORK)

BLOOPER VIDEO

Take the edge off enjoying these sports or outdoor adventure videos. This is an inexpensive and entertaining gift for all ages that results in laughter. They say laughter is the best medicine. Check you local video stores for sales and online video stores as well. You'll have hours of laughter and entertainment at a low price.

A great guy gift is a favorite old movie of his. Ask your man what one of his favorite movies is and you can pick most of them up on DVD now, for under $10.00."

--QUINN BRINKERHOFF
(ST. GEORGE, UTAH)

FLASHLIGHT

His flashlight always seems to disappear! Purchase two this time so he has one for back up. You may want to add his name to it or a notes that says something like, "Only touch if you're DAD!"

Jerky is a great snack for people who want to add protein to their diet. It is also a great snack and meal replacement for those watching carbs. Guys love it and there are some great flavors like Grilled Steak, Teriyaki, Sizzle Beef, and Tex Mex. Great Lakes Jerky out of Michigan has 27 flavors available and vacuum packed shipping available to assure freshness. A special treat for your man!
- MIKE CURTIS
(GRAND HAVEN, MICHIGAN)

CHAPTER NINE:
QUICK THANK-YOU GIFTS

What do you do when a card just isn't enough to say "thank you"? In the next few pages, we'll give you some ideas of how to say it through eloquent and caring gifts, gifts that show that your gratitude is truly from the heart.

TAKE A BREAK

A fabulous way to show appreciation is to fill a gift bag with a game like Yahtzee or a movie, package of popcorn, two liter bottle of soda and a bag of M&Ms along with a gift tag that reads, "Take a break on us!" or, "Have a fun family evening & Thank You for all you have done!"

I like to give a card organizer as a gift. Hallmark currently has one and it includes dividers for different occasions as well as months of the year that you can write birthdays etc. I purchase a variety of cards for each category such as sympathy, congratulations, baby, wedding as well as pretty notepaper, stickers for decorating the envelopes and stamps (useful for elderly). Friends are even requesting this gift.

- AZANA JOHNSON
(ROSEVILLE, CALIFORNIA)

GIFT CARDS

Add a simple gift certificate for something creative and enjoyable to a personalized thank-you note.

Afew simple, yet well appreciated ideas are:

- Latte
- Dozen donuts
- Fast Food
- Manicure
- Dozen tulips

Clean out three matching salsa or mayonnaise jars. Remove labels and add sand in the bottom of the jar, a couple of shells, stones or marbles. Add a scented tea light candle. Put them in a box with a big bow and your recipient will have a great new set of candles for a mantle or shelf.

- BRIDGET RIETH
(GRAND RAPIDS, MICHIGAN)

GERANIUM

A great gift at a great price because geraniums are among the few flowers that grow almost anywhere! They are inexpensive and much appreciated.

A few years ago, as part of my business, I had placed a facial box in a local store where women could register for a free facial. I set up an appointment over the phone with one particular lady who had registered (I'll call her "Ruth"). Upon arriving for our appointment, I found she lived in a shabby old mobile home in a rough neighborhood. Ruth was a tired-looking, bony little woman who looked much older than her years but she was warm and courteous...she told me she used only soap and water and had never worn makeup, so I gave her the works - foundation, lipstick, blush, everything in my bag! She looked so pretty, and was absolutely delighted at her transformation and so grateful to me...my heart went out to her and found myself wanting to give her something special but could tell that —though poor— she was proud. So I found myself asking her to enter my no-purchase-necessary drawing for a FREE Pampering Spa set (there was no drawing, at least not until that moment). Well, she "won" the drawing, and when I delivered her gift, the look of true gratitude on her face was a humble reminder to me of how easily one can be tempted to judge others by outward appearances. In that single moment, without even knowing it, she became the gift-giver!

- SHARON HEDGE
(FOLEY, MISSOURI)

NOVEL & BOOKMARK

A recent bestseller and bookmark is a terrific thank-you that will last longer than a day. This is a great gift for a friend and to give during the holidays. Here are a few simple and touching readers:

* Skipping Christmas - John Grisham
* Angels Everywhere - Debbie Macomber
* A Gift to Last - Debbie Macomber
* Anything by Nicholas Sparks

My daughter and I went to town to run errands and on the way she surprised me with a visit for a manicure. It sure made me feel special!

- NINA DENZIN
(CLYDE PARK, MONTANA)

CHOCOLATE

Who doesn't love a giant Hershey bar? Add a sticky note to the top with your thank-you and you will see a smile! A very quick and fun gift for under $2.oo! Why not? Give one today and see the reaction for yourself!

Romantic memories? When I first met me husband, we went to see the movie Titanic. I was so moved by it that my husband found a picture of the famous couple standing on the ledge of the boat and framed it for me along with the lyrics of the song "My heart will go on." This gift didn't cost much but it meant a lot to me because he took the time to make it and it came from the heart!

*- APRIL GRAVETT
(ELIZABETHTOWN, KENTUCKY)*

CUP OF TEA

Add a few tea packets and a cute or fancy teaspoon to a teacup. Tea is one of those relaxing treats that many could use. Consider adding a cute little honey bear to the center of the tea cup and then wrap it in cellophane. Add a personal note expressing your thanks for a very elegant gift.

I make many gifts for relatives and family members and quite enjoy it. Some ideas include incense, homemade bath salts (my favorite) and homemade salt scrubs. Gift jars can be made very easily buying mason jars in a case and make them all in one batch for many people! Hot Cocoa Gift Jars, Cookie Gift Jars and Coffee Gift Jars are among my favorites! All of these are relatively inexpensive and you can find recipes for all the above gifts on the Internet. Once made, they appear to be very expensive, unique and made by you!
- ASHLEY STALLINGS
(KINGSTON, NORTH CAROLINA)

CANDY DISH

Paint a terra cotta pot a solid color, then add painted polka dots or flowers with another bright color. Once it dries, place a bright-colored ribbon around the top of the dish and fill it with candy. Wrap your pot in a cellophane bag, tying the top with curling ribbon. These pots can be purchased as low as 50 cents and have lots of potential for gifts!

I like to do this one for teachers and new mothers, who tend to be under stress and have little time for themselves. I go to the Dollar Tree or other everything-is-one-dollar store and buy a basket, some bath scrubbies, some votive candles, and manicure items. I will spend a little more at a drug or discount store for nail polish, bubble bath, and lotion. I make a "spa treatment" basket by putting the scrubbies in the bottom of the basket, then arranging the other items (I wrap the votives in mesh and tie them with satin ribbon for a little frill, and I have been known to tie them with twine or jute to follow the mood of the basket). Usually it isn't necessary to wrap this up in cello, though I did thirty of these for teachers and I wrapped them to make transportation easier. I put a gift tag on there with a little poem or short note about how they are so great and deserve to take a moment to relax. This basket costs about $10 on average to put together, and the response is overwhelming. When I did the ones for the teachers, I managed to spend less than $200 for thirty baskets.

- TIFFANY CLEMMONS
(POWHATAN, VIRGINIA)

CHAPTER TEN:
SPECIAL EVENTS

There are times in our lives when we just want to give a little more, do something out of the ordinary or join in on the expense of a gift with others. Here are some great ideas that been a big hit for many!

WEDDING EXTRAVAGANZA

Pitch in with friends to pay for the wedding night hotel room. The hotel can assist you in sending an order of chocolate-covered strawberries and a bottle of champagne to their room as a special surprise they will always remember.

I came up with this idea in honor of my in-laws' 50th wedding anniversary. Can you imagine sharing 50 years together? That deserves a celebration! Here was my idea. Set up the reception area by decorating each table to signify an event or activity in their lives. Each table can be decorated with a tablecloth, then the theme is added. Drape either a clear tablecloth over the top or a glass top. For example, their first date was to the release of Disney's Snow White so one table was a Snow White children's table cloth with movie release posters. One table was all photos of their grandchildren and another of saved artwork that their own children had created in school. My father-in-law was a star athlete in high school, so one table was photos and old newspaper articles from football, basketball, and when he and his teammates were inducted into the Hall of Fame at age 70! My mother-in-law spent 20 years volunteering with the church's Angel Choir. So one table held her favorite sheet music, photos and notes written by past students. You can also take some bulky items from their past and create a "time-line" down the buffet table.

The key is to really think of them, their lives, and what they value from their lives. Scrap booking supplies are ideal to help present themes. The guests will mingle so well, looking from table to table; and the guests of honor will be just that, honored.

- SHAUNNA BERGLUND (HELENA, MONTANA)

TEEN CELEBRATION

Tell your teens to get dressed up and ready for a night on the town in style. Hire a limousine to pick the teens up and take them to dinner or to a movie. Make sure you leave a few spare moments on the ride to stop by a few places such as a convenience store. The teens will want to be seen in their cool ride!

When I was a teenager (1941), we lived in a small community of about 200 people. Cubb Creek, Tennessee, was a rural area with about 15 teenagers, and other than church there wasn't much for us to do. The Pearl Harbor attack had a big effect on us, and our mothers wanted to do something for us that didn't involve a lot of money or extravagant things. They got together and decided to have a Sunday dinner just for us teenagers, rotating houses every Sunday. One mother had an organ, playing after dinner while we all gathered around and sang songs. Sometimes we played croquet or games. I'll never forget when it was Mama's turn for dinner; she put her white linen table cloth on the table and used her best dishes. I remember the Kool Aid and iced tea on those hot summer days. This was a very special memory for the teenagers and a special gift from our mothers!

- WILLIE MAE REEVES
(COOKEVILLE, TENNESSEE)

FOR ANYONE

Do you know someone who has a special wish? Help make someone's dream come true. Send them to a sporting event or sign them up for a class they have always dreamed of attending. If the expense is too high, then ask family or friends to help out. This takes a little thought and a few secrets have to be kept to pull it off, but it is truly rewarding. You can do anything you put your mind to!

One of the things that I find very fun to give during Christmas time and that really gets the kids involved is my stocking stuffer gift. These are great for the "hard to buy for" and for grandparents. You can obtain many of these items at a thrift shop or on bargain racks in any store: Christmas stockings, bows, ribbons, glitter (several colors), colored paper (or card stock), glue, and crayons.

Let the kids make Christmas cards with the color paper, glitter and crayons. They can add bows and ribbon for that special touch too. Use the remaining glitter and ribbon to create a unique stocking. Add something like the grandchildren's names and put "To Our #1 Grandma" etc. Stuff the stockings with a mixture of items. Here are a few examples: sample soaps, laundry detergent, makeup, toothpaste or travel items Christmas candies; hard candy, chocolate, nuts, items that are unique to your town or area; foods, flowers, sauces, soup mixes and candles.

Every time I give these away at Christmas time, the receiver goes nuts! They love the idea that the kids were a part of it and it came from the heart. You can also use two pieces of felt to make a stocking and put together with shoestrings. Cost: $15-20

- KELLY TAYLOR (ROCKY FORD, COLORADO)

KIDS

Get a hotel room! The kids will love to swim until late, and you can pick up cheese or pepperoni pizzas to take to the room and keep expenses down. Give the kids a disposable camera along with a photo album from the dollar store so they can keep their memories alive. This type of party or event is often cheaper than many others when comparing to an amusement park or restaurant.

For a simple and inexpensive child's gift, wrap a few coloring books and crayons in the Sunday funny papers. Kids never have enough coloring books and crayons and they will love the look of the wrap!

- NANCY MALTAIS
(GILMANTON IRONWORKS, NEW HAMPSHIRE)

SLUMBER PARTY KIT

For a special birthday, let them plan a slumber birthday! The kids always seem to ask for these parties and parents hesitate because of the chaos and the thought of being up all night. Ugh! Be on top of it this time giving them everything they need to have that fun sleep-over. Pack a box for the birthday person to open and include:

- Plain white pillow cases
- Markers for autograph fun to decorate the cases
- A special movie to watch
- A board or card game
- 5 small prizes wrapped up for the game winners
- Lots of snacks

For great gifts by kids; purchase a picture frame and add their picture. Let the kids add potpourri, shells, small rocks, gems etc. with glue, making a decorative frame for a gift many will adore!

- SHEILA SKUDALSKI
(LITTLE EGG HARBOR, NEW JERSEY)

THE HAVE-TOS

There are many things in life that we don't like to do, but that we have to. Give someone a helping hand with some of these ideas:

* Vehicle oil change
* Window washing
* Put up their Christmas lights
* Carpet cleaning
* Auto detail
* House cleaning
* Mow the lawn

One Christmas I was given a lovely little household toolbox including a small hammer, tape measure, screwdrivers, wrenches etc. When I opened it up, I found a cartoon series taped on the inside cover titled "Love Is."

The cartoon showed a character saying, "I Love You." I always thought that my former husband had taped it in the box, but found out years later that it was my young daughter who had.

The gift alone was a wonderful, inexpensive gift and to know that my daughter was involved gives me goose bumps every time I recall the memory.

- PAT GALLOWAY
(SCOTTSBURG, OREGON)

THROW A PARTY

For no reason at all! Parties, friends and get-togethers make life fun. Here are a few party ideas for any age:

Tea party

Buffet style dinner

Mystery dinner

Holiday charity party - A very meaningful party with a little pizzazz! Each attendee brings an item to fill a stocking for needy children or bake cakes for your local homeless shelter. Of course you add a little fun and games too like a door prize for all attendees. This party has been given for both adults and children. It is easy to plan and promotes community involvement.

Breakfast party - People get together frequently for dinner, but what about breakfast? Do something out of the norm! This is a great get together. Serve fruits, juices and croissants. Give everyone a rolled up newspaper at their place setting.

For each birthday, ask the child to choose what will be served for dinner to the family on his/her birthday - they can choose their favorite foods. This will make the child feel special!

- HEIDI SALTER
(YPSILANTI, MICHIGAN)

CHAPTER ELEVEN: GIFTS FOR ANYONE, AT ANY TIME

There is often a time in a person's life when they want to give a gift "just because," or possibly for an event out of the ordinary. The following ideas may just be the ticket!

FUN WITH FRUIT

A freshly-filled fruit bowl is such an eye-appealing treat. You can purchase a wire-footed basket at your local department store. Fill with colorful fresh fruits for a great gift!

At the age of 7, I was lucky to have neighbors that had a raspberry bush and allowed me to pick all of them I could eat. One day, I thought that I needed to thank them for their generosity so, I went across the street and picked a bunch of raspberries from their bush and took them home. Mom and Dad were at work, and I figured I could be a baker. I was going to make them a raspberry pie. Well, I had seen my mom do it many times. I remember putting lots of sugar in the raspberries, then making a crust (I had to go to borrow an egg from my neighbors). I didn't have enough to make a regular pie so I cut one of Mom's pie tins and made a small one, then baked it. I then took it to my neighbor friends. My mom came home and saw the flour mess and was a little upset, and asked what I had done. I told her that I made a pie for our neighbors, and she gasped (knowing I did not know how to bake a pie). She went over and asked them if they had eaten it yet, and the neighbor told her "Well (with a sheepish grin) I thought I would wait for Ernie (her husband) to get home and have the first bite"...I never did find out how that pie turned out, but I did receive friends for LIFE."
    Memories of gift giving built by love and kindness!

- TONYA WOOD
(KIT CARSON, COLORADO)

PINS

Fun and funky hat and coat pins are fun to give! You can purchase bright rhinestone pins in the shapes of animals to cars for under $10.00. Add them to a sheer organza bag for an elegant look.

In my business, I sell scarves and pin sets for under $10.00. My customers come back time and time again telling me how much their recipient loved them. It is a simple yet classy gift to give!
- INTERNET GIFT SELLER

AN EMERGENCY CAR KIT IS A PRACTICAL GIFT
FOR NEW CAR DRIVERS.

SPICE IT UP

Spices are something we use almost every day, but have you ever received them as a gift? What a treat! Go to a health food store and purchase three different spices, putting them in small containers as a gift. There is nothing like fresh organic spices!

Here is a simple gift idea that many will enjoy making and giving!

Fragrance Stones
1 1/2 cups flour
1/4 cup of salt
1/4 tsp. cornstarch
2/3 cup of boiling water
1 TBS. of fragrance oil (get this at a health food store, or craft store like Michael's)
Color choice (use spices, cocoa, wear gloves with food coloring.)

Mix all the dry ingredients together. Heat water in the microwave or stove, add the fragrance and color to the water. Stir water mixture into the flour mixture. Mix as best as you can, then knead the dough. You want it to look like pie or cookie dough.

Roll out 1/4 inch thick and cut into shapes, or form it into balls. Then let air dry till it is hard. You have an air freshener or scented ornaments for holiday or gifts. You could punch a small hole into it and add a small ribbon for hanging on a tree, or door, or a suction cup for sticking to a window.

- CATHY LEEDY
(NORTH WEBSTER, INDIANA)

ENTERTAINING GIFT IDEA

If you are visiting someone's home and would like to bring a thank-you gesture; try this:

Take a small cutting board and add a small box of crackers, package of cheese and summer sausage on top of the board. Wrap with ribbon, holding the items in place. This is also a nice gift for travel, thank-you and get well.

For my birthday, my friend packed a picnic basket, and told me to meet her at 12:00 noon out in front of my workplace. She proceeded to take me to a nearby park, and pulled out a lunch - complete with blanket to put down - and we had a lovely time. It was one of the nicest birthday presents I ever received!

- PATRICIA O'DONNELL
(HAVERTOWN, PENNSYLVANIA)

HEART AND SOUL

If you really want to put your heart into it, express it in a letter. Throughout our lives we are blessed with friends and family who show their love in many different ways. There is something very special about reading a personal letter given to you that expresses love. Tell them how proud you are of them regarding a personal achievement or a letter of appreciation to a dear friend. If you don't mind your letter being read by others, put it in a photo frame prior to giving.

My favorite gift idea to give my family and friends is a 100% thick cotton pillowcase with a printed design, or a 100% thick cotton flannel sheet blanket (like you would find in the hospital). People love super-soft blankets, and pillows are loved by all!
- BARBARA NYSWONGER
(NEW CUYAMA, CALIFORNIA)

HOUSEHOLD KEY ORGANIZER

Make labeled key chains to help folks get organized. Attach them to a magnetic hook to put on the refrigerator, thus eliminating the hunt! This is especially a great helper for the elderly.

I recently attended a quilt retreat and while I was there I found some fabric that really called out to me. I bought only a yard of it because it was expensive and I didn't know how I was going to use it. Then it dawned on me what to do. I took the frame from a painting that I had picked up at a yard sale for $3.00. I framed a quarter yard of the fabric in the frame and put it up in my sewing room. The total cost was only $8.50 and I love looking at this unique print! What a great gift this would be for the person that appreciates fabric or quilting.

- MAGGIE HAILE
(NAMPA, IDAHO)

BASKET OF FUN

A fun favorite! Take a small basket or container and fill it with about 10 small wrapped gifts. Wrap each gift in different papers, colored wrap, tissues, gift bags, cellophane bags etc. It takes a little thought but it is entertaining, bright and fun for the recipient. Fun to make too! Items can be as simple as the following:

• Pocket calendar	• Chewing gum
• Candy Bar	• Pill box
• Chap Stick	• Mini cookbook
• Writing pen	• Stylish sticky notes
• Nail polish	• One pot coffee packet
• Notepad	• Hand lotion
• Flashlight	• Nail file
• Hair Brush/Comb	• Bath gel
• Candle	• Deck of cards
• Earrings	• Garden seeds
• Magazine	• Crossword Puzzle Book

A gift that I received from my daughter was a single blade pocket knife that was an old timer. I am not sure of the cost but it is small and a gift that I will always treasure.

- QUINN BRINKERHOFF
(ST. GEORGE, UTAH)

MEMORABLE PHOTOS

A black-and-white photo is a treasure, as it is so different from a color photo. Expressions of the person will show more than the background color effects you find in traditional film. Purchase a roll of black-and-white film and take pictures of your children for a great Christmas present for relatives.

One year I asked my son for a pair of old horse shoe book ends with our brand in the center. He was surprised that this was all I wanted, and these book ends are a proud possession of my many that didn't cost anything.
- NINA DENZIN
(CLYDE PARK, MONTANA)

BRIGHTEN THEIR DAY

Surprise them with a simple note left on their car under the windshield wiper. It can be as simple as "I Love You," or "Have a Great Day!" This can mean so much and it doesn't cost a cent.

I find baskets at garage sales, rummage sales and from friends and neighbors. I rarely spend more than $.50 per basket. I clean them and spray paint them white, then spray paint them again yellow. There are 3 groups of items included in each basket. Useful items such as a comb, emery board, tissues, hand sanitizer, nail clipper, chap stick, perfume or aftershave samples, hair bands or clips, note pad, pen, tooth brush. A fun item such as a crossword puzzle book or word find, a small stuffed animal, small figurine, deck of cards, small calculator, hand made items, small silk flowers. The third item is an inspirational item such as a devotional booklet, Cross in My Pocket with corresponding poem, tracts, etc., and each basket contains an angel. I wrap each basket with cellophane and tie with a big pull type bow.

I deliver them to a hospital as well as a nursing home here in Cincinnati. The chaplain or nurse decides who will get them. Sometimes I am treated to a heart-warming story about a recipient of a basket. However, this is done completely anonymously on both sides. I have so much fun shopping for items, and finding new things to include in the baskets. I also have some very dear friends who give me items for the baskets. It is a very rewarding project for me and I know it is appreciated!

- ARLENE JONES
(CINCINNATI, OHIO)

BOOKMARK IT

This is a special gift that can become a very fulfilling project. Make individual bookmarks using cardstock paper or purchasing pre-cut marks that also come with tassels from your local craft store. Add items such as sayings, personal written messages, lace, buttons, and scrapbooking items. Once you have completed your bookmark, laminate it with inexpensive laminate sheets on the front and back. Punch a hole in the top and add ribbon or a tassel. This is a perfect holiday gift to add to your Christmas greeting card as a meaningful gift.

Several years back I had an employee whose five-year anniversary was coming up and I had no idea what to give him. This is a person who has everything, eats consciously and enjoys the finer things in life. I decided to do something simple and out of the ordinary putting emphasis on him and his five years of service instead of the gift. The first thing I did was put five balloons in his office, added a few streamers to his desk and a simple sign that said "5 years!" Throughout the day, I kept referring to the number five, giving him small gifts like five granola bars wrapped up in a cellophane bag. Another gift was five notepads with his name on the top to use in the office. For lunch we had his wife come over for a surprise lunch and at the end of the day gave him five lottery tickets. This can be done for many different occasions such as a birthday. It didn't cost much and someone felt like a king for the entire day!
- LONNA WEIDEMANN
(HELENA, MONTANA)

TREASURED TIMES

Make someone else's life easier by passing along the fun of "Treasured Times". Share the stories and great ideas with a friend!

Here is an idea that is great for a Christmas gift: hand-painted snowman head ornaments made from a simple salt dough recipe. I sold over 900 of these ornaments on the Internet. A few folks were repeat buyers. I also made a few sets for my son's teachers for him to give to them at their Christmas party.

Simple Salt Dough Recipe:
1 cup all purpose flour, sifted
1/2 - 3/4 cup lukewarm water
1 cup salt

Mix all ingredients in a medium-sized bowl. Roll dough out with rolling pin. Cut circles about 2" in diameter (I used the round lid top to my cooking spray to make the circles). Lay the cut circles out on a cookie sheet (spray with cooking spray, if needed). Take a straw and poke holes at the tops of the circles. This is so you can hang the ornaments. Then bake at 300 degrees for 30 - 40 minutes. Take out of oven and let them cool.

Materials: Paint brush, white, orange and black acrylic paints, and spray sealant (about $3-4 at Wal-Mart).Paint the ornaments white, let dry. Paint the mouth and eyes black using dots for the eye and mouth. Paint on a carrot nose, using a triangle shape with a rounded end. Once they are completely dry, spray the sealant on the front. When dries, turn over and spray the back.

A very easy and very inexpensive gift!
- MARCIE CLEVELAND
(HARTWELL, GEORGIA)

GOURMET COFFEES

There are a lot of coffee drinkers these days, but they rarely buy the good stuff for themselves. A bag of gourmet coffee is a gift you can give for many reasons. Consider the following brands for a rich pot of brew! Just add a bow and gift card.

- Peet's Coffee
- Godiva
- Starbucks
- Pampered Chef

Many of these can be purchased at your local grocery store or department store.

A decorative potpourri bowl is an inexpensive gift that people really love receiving. Purchase an ivy bowl that is 4" in diameter, then fill it with potpourri, add a 6" lace crocheted doily on top of it, then a rubber band on the neck of bowl to hold the doily in place. Put ribbon over the rubber band around the neck of the bowl leaving tails of 3-4" long to make a bow or tie ends in a knot leaving tails hanging. Sometimes I give the like bottle of the potpourri scent so they can add a couple of drops through the doily then they don't have to take the whole thing apart to change the potpourri.

- WENDY PATRICK
(COLORADO SPRINGS, COLORADO)

$2.49 VALUE

A value for $2.49? It's true! You can do it using videotapes and a little of your time. Here are two different versions, both tried and tested as big hits!

- I am sure you have many friends or relatives that that have very busy schedules and do not have time to watch daytime television. A great gift is to tape a show such as Oprah or a car race. Wrap it up and add a note card letting them know that this gift was made especially for them to relax and enjoy! All it takes is a blank video!

- For a distant friend or relative, make a family video. Your first instinct is to think about how long it will take to pull this off. Not true! Follow this method for an easy, inexpensive gift for all! If you do not own a video recorder, ask to borrow a friend's for a day. Title your video "From our home to yours" or "A day in the life at our house." Simply start in the morning and record bits and pieces all day. Tell them what day of the week it is, what the plan is for the day, get a glimpse of the kids eating breakfast, in their room, the pets, the house and don't forget to have someone video you also! If you go to a sporting event or anywhere else for the day, take the camera with you. Show new prized possessions you have purchased or received as gifts. Let your family enjoy opening this home made video with excitement! You'll be glad you did! Check your local Costco, BJ's, or Sam's Club for great deals on blank videos in bulk. They will cost around $2.00 apiece!

- This is a great idea for a new grandparent to do for Mom and Dad. Each time you have that lovely new baby over; take a few video clips for the first six to twelve months. Then wrap the videos up in a pink or blue ribbon (whichever is appropriate) and give them to Mon and Dad as a very special Christmas present they will forever treasure.

A Pampered Chef Ice Cream dipper is a special gift for the ice cream fan! It contains a defrosting fluid making scooping easy! It even has a warranty. Your recipient won't cringe next time the ice cream is hard and they can't seem to get it out of the box!

- LONNA WEIDEMANN (HELENA, MONTANA)

A FINAL FEW IDEAS

The best gift I ever received was from two ladies friends of mine. They gave me a covered candy dish that was filled with 100 small slips of paper. On each piece of paper was a wish or wise saying designed to make me smile or give my day a lift. Friendly wishes. The instructions told me that each time I was feeling down or having a bad day I was to reach in, pull one out and read it aloud to myself, or share it with anyone around me who also might need to smile. I kept that jar on my desk for years, and just knowing it was there, even if I didn't pull one out to read it, made me feel better. When I did pull one out to read it, I was touched by their effort. They made sure that the last little piece of paper was taped to the bottom of the jar (so I wouldn't pull it out accidentally before my jar was empty) and it asked me to pass the jar on.

It just so happened that I had recently made a new friend who was having a birthday the following week. I had been struggling on a gift, not knowing her tastes, yet wanting to show her that her friendship was a welcome addition to my life. I hesitated for only a moment, selfishly not wanting to give away my beautiful little dish. I then set to the task of cutting strips of pretty paper and enjoying myself completely, thinking up things to write to her. I actually ended up with more than 100 wishes, and I remembered to tape the first one (last one) to the bottom of the jar, asking her to pass it on. I found out much later that she did and I know it has gone further than that. It was a gift I will never forget and have made new ones for others.

- JOY EARLS
(BURNSIDE, KENTUCKY)

When my grandson graduated from high school, I pulled him aside and said, "I know this isn't much, but I think it's something you might need." It was a subscription to the Wall Street Journal. I handed it to him and he put it down and said, "Thanks, I'll read that later." I told him he really should take a look at it right then. He opened the newspaper and his expression turned to one of delight. I had taped money ($1.00, $5.00 and other bills) throughout the newspaper. As he turned the pages, the bills got bigger. Not only did he get a great paper that would help his future, but he also had some immediate cash to boot.

- NORMAN WITHERBEE
(HELENA, MONTANA)

The Dollar Stores out there these days are great assets for any gift-giver: with just a little imagination, you can give great gifts for very little money. I once made closet and drawer pomanders for a friend who had just bought a home, where the previous owner was a smoker and her financial situation would not allow her to do heavy renovation. So I bought some tulle netting circles (the kind brides use for their favors), and made up a simple potpourri of old rose petals and dried botanicals around my home, crushed them by hand, added a few tiny artificial flowers I had on a sprig lying around, mixed the lot with about 8-12 drops of Essential Oil to scent. We tied the little bundles closed with raffia scraps I had left over from a previous project, and stuck the same tiny flowers from the plastic sprig I had in the knot of the raffia, and gave her about 20 of these that she could stick into drawers, closets, and set out in a bowl for scenting the air. It did the trick.

SANDRA HOLMAN
(STOCKTON, CALIFORNIA)

Another inexpensive gift idea is making your own carpet sprinkle for vacuuming away odors and bringing a great scent into the home. Mix two cups of baking soda in a glass or metal bowl or canning jar with at least two inches of space above the top, add several drops of fragrance oil or CLEAR essential oil due to the fact that some essential oils have a yellow color, stir by hand until well mixed, and put into any powder or spice container with a shaker top or, if you are creative, a decorative canning jar with holes poked through the lid with a nail for sprinkling on the carpet just prior to vacuuming.

- SANDRA HOLMAN
(STOCKTON, CALIFORNIA)

I make vintage doll trunks with a baby doll, clothes, shoes, blankets etc. It can be difficult to keep the little outfits organized, so I use little clothespins to hold the non-hanging outfits together. You can purchase smaller clothes hangers and clothespins at department and craft stores. This is a great way to give some doll clothes, or for the doll collector to stay organized.

- LAURA WALL
(MORRIS, ILLINOIS)

This is an idea for teachers and classmates for an end-of-the-school-year gift. I am creating a personalized word search or crossword puzzle, which is a program that you can find on the Internet (or make up your own). I am getting my children's classmate list and/or words that describe the school year. Then I am titling it "My Fourth Grade" or "Class of 2003-2004," adding a border and rolling it up like a scroll. Then I'll tie ribbon around it or buy a picture frame to give one to the teacher as a memorabilia/keepsake along with my children's name on it as the one who created it. The teachers and students will enjoy doing this puzzle that is all about them!

- ANNETTE RAMIREZ
(SAN DIMAS, CALIFORNIA)

Being an only child, my son (now three), is the only grandchild, great-nephew, and great-grandson on my side of the family. For Christmas one year, I bought aprons and painted everyone's first name on them. I let my 18-month-old do hand prints (when he'd do them) or just gave him paint brushes and let the apron be his canvas. I started in October, and only did a few at a time; when the Michaels craft store coupons came out I would buy an apron, so they would cost about $2.75 each. This was a huge hit for the family members! Everyone still wears them!

Another year I sent out a letter in July with a self-addressed envelope and asked for everyone to mail me a appetizer, a main dish and a dessert recipe along with family favorite pictures. I then started collecting the coupons again in the paper and bought small spiral scrap books and entered the recipes on my computer and scanned in the pictures, made copies, and made labels that said "From the Kitchen of Aunt Wendy" (or whomever) and put it on the appropriate page. That way, everyone knew whose special recipe it was. We used craft scalloped scissors and glued all the recipes and picture in the book. That was the hit at Christmas - no one else opened any presents that night, they all had such a blast looking at the pictures! My aunt and I had fun making these since we got to pick and choose the photos.

- *PEPPER NINIS*
(ST. PETE, FLORIDA)

When my son was a junior or senior in high school, he wrote me a poem and framed it and gave it to me for Mothers' Day with a very nice card. I still have it framed and on my dresser 17 years later. It brought tears to my eyes then as it still does today when I read it. I was a single mom struggling financially to raise two kids and we didn't have much money, but we had a lot of love. This is what it says:

MOM
As I grow wise with age (so I hope),
I think of all you've done for me.
My impatience, my frustration,
(with which you cope)
With such grace and reasonability.

I know it's been tough, supporting us two, the
dollars not half what
it was.
Yet whenever I needed, I came to you
and you gave what you had "just because".

So I 'd like to now extend,
a heartfelt "thanks" from us two.
And I'm sorry that it's been
So long that I've said
"I LOVE YOU!"
Storm

- CJ SHOUMAN
(KENT, WASHINGTON)

RESOURCES FOR GIFTS

Michaels Crafts

Creative Bookmark Ideas
www.Michaels.com
Enter bookmark under search

Lillian Vernon

Personalized Pencils
Lillian Vernon Corp.
100 Lillian Vernon Dr.
Virginia Beach, VA 23479
800-901-9291
www.lillianvernon.com

Amazon

Bloopers Videos
www.amazon.com

Current Inc.

Personalized Notepads
Homeowners Diary
Current USA Inc.
1005 East Woodmen Road
Colorado Springs, CO 80920
877-655-4458
www.currentcatalog.com

E-Bay

Creative Gifts
www.ebay.com

Createforless

Crafting Source/Craft Kits
www.createforless.com
866-333-4463

CONTRIBUTORS

Denise Delsman
Christine Beers
Ann Tanner
Deb Solberg
Jessica Cobia
Linda McNeece
Christi Narron
Bea Jacobs
Kathi Brady
Catherine Donelan
Gloria McMican
Nancy Bridenbaker
Darla Agtarap
Tonya Johnson
Kerri Freundschuh
Mtn. View Hypnotherapy
Nancy Maltais
Janessa Butterfield
Tricia Schmitz
Kimberly Vetrano
Kristin Prestholdt Johnshoy
Melissa Samatas
Azana Johnson
Tassie Dimmitt
Norm Witherbee
Lisa Jewett
Evan Krichman

Debbie Krivanec
Sharon St. Pierre
Beth Lesher
Larry Pfeil
Alison Richmond
Angie Mew
Krista Hinchey
Wendy Woods
Cathy Funderburg
Cassandra Norton
Yvonne Wiltshire
Kate Falvey
Linda Raynovic
Tiffany Clemmons
Lucy Leon
Kathy Oakes
Lorri Jones
Heidi Thompson
Tracey Sharis
Tina Wisely
Jessica Christensen
Jennifer Pattison
Joy Earls
Amy Ulibarri
CJ Shouman
Heide Salter
Kathy Davenport

Dennis Fournier
Steve Hickman
Trudy Sarata
Mike Curtis
Sharon Hedge
April Gravett
Shaunna Berglund
Kelly Taylor
Pat Galloway
Cathy Leedy
Maggie Haile
Marcie Cleveland
Jenny Partnier

Brenda Worcester
Eric Brown
Quinn Brinkerhoff
Bridget Rieth
Nina Denzin
Ashley Stallings
Willie Mae Reeves
Sheila Skudalski
Tonya Wood
Patricia O'Donnell
Arlene Jones
Wendy Patrick

Fun & Friendly Templates

Feel free to use these templates for your gift-giving by simply making a photocopy and adding them to your gift. We just ask that you use them for personal gift-giving as they are not intended for business use.

Here are a few tips to help make your templates fun & friendly:

- Use colored paper when making photocopies.
- Increase the size for larger templates.
- Use markers and stickers to brighten them up

A Simple Gift Tag

A Gift For You!

To: _____

From: _____

TEACHER THANK-YOUS

1. Use a 4"x 9" cellophane bag (or use a larger one, trimming it down).
2. Add a teacher notepad inside or a pad of post it notes.
3. Lay a pencil on the top of the cellophane bag in vertical position.
4. Bunch the center of the bag together with a piece of curling ribbon (holding the pencil in place on the outside) and add a whole punch to the tag to attach to the front. Draw it all together and tie in a knot.
5. Curl your ribbon.

Thanks for being a great teacher!

To: _____

From: _____

COUPONS FOR ALL!

You read it over and over. Coupons are a big hit! Here is a simple coupon you can use for anyone, decorating as you wish. It is fun to write the word "never" in the expiration field.

This coupon is good for:

To:

From:

Expires:

AFTERWORD

Always remember to use your heart and thoughts when it comes to a special gift. It is the fact that you are doing something for someone else that matters, not how expensive it is!

TREASURED TIMES SERIES

Filled to the brim with gift ideas for under $10.00, adding a splash of fun using simple ideas from the heart and not the pocketbook. An inspiration and practical guide for all walks of life. Sit down with a cup of tea and enjoy the stories from real people, recounting the most memorable gifts they've given or received in their life, and sharing ideas for everyone to use!

Look forward to this future title in our series:

- **Playing For Keeps: Building Memories With Your Kids** – Full of fun and creative ideas to use with children. From simple boredom busters, and a Christian Corner chapter, to the foods they love and more!

ORDER FORM

Fax Orders		(406) 449-4711	
Phone Orders		(406) 431-4180	
On-Line Orders		www.lwpromo.com	
Postal Orders		LW Promotionals	
		P.O. Box 7583	
		Helena, MT 59604	

QTY	Item	Price	Extension
	101 Creative Gift Ideas Under $10	$12.99	
		Subtotal	
Shipping: $3 for first book, $1.50 for each additional book			
		Total	

Payment: Check or Money Order ____
          Credit Card _Visa__M/C__Amex__Discover

Card Number: _____

Expiration date: _____/_____

Name on card: _____

Ship to:

Name: _____

Address _____

_____

City _____ State _____ Zip _____

Phone _____

Email _____

ORDER FORM

Fax Orders	(406) 449-4711
Phone Orders	(406) 431-4180
On-Line Orders	www.lwpromo.com
Postal Orders	LW Promotionals
	P.O. Box 7583
	Helena, MT 59604

QTY	Item	Price	Extension
	101 Creative Gift Ideas Under $10	$12.99	
	Subtotal		
	Shipping: $3 for first book, $1.50 for each additional book		
	Total		

Payment: Check or Money Order ___
            Credit Card _Visa__M/C__Amex__Discover

Card Number: _____

Expiration date: _____/_____

Name on card: _____

Ship to:

Name: _____

Address _____

_____

City _____ State _____ Zip _____

Phone _____

Email _____

Printed in the United States
86671LV00005B/199-225/A